W9-CLQ-961

LIFE LESSONS FROM THE OLDEST AND WISEST

*Inspiration, Wisdom, and
Humor for All Generations*

DAVID ROMANELLI

Skyhorse Publishing

Skyhorse Publishing books may be purchased in bulk at special discounts for sales promotion, corporate gifts, fund-raising, or educational purposes. Special editions can also be created to specifications. For details, contact the Special Sales Department, Skyhorse Publishing, 307 West 36th Street, 11th Floor, New York, NY 10018 or info@skyhorsepublishing.com.

Skyhorse® and Skyhorse Publishing® are registered trademarks of Skyhorse Publishing, Inc.®, a Delaware corporation.

Visit our website at www.skyhorsepublishing.com.

10 9 8 7 6 5 4 3 2 1

Library of Congress Cataloging-in-Publication Data is available on file.

Cover design by Rose Leopold
Cover photo by Norberto Rodriguez

Print ISBN: 978-1-5107-3659-7
Ebook ISBN: 978-1-5107-3662-7

Printed in the United States of America

DEDICATION

To my grandparents, Evelyn and Joe, Neda and Bert: every day, I think about when we played catch and went fishing, ate gnocchi for lunch and cremadoro for dessert, and shared long conversations snacking on bagel chips at a Jewish deli. How much I have missed you and how excited I am to see you again.

To my children, Remo and Cooper: cherish your grandparents. Be grateful for their kindness and patience. Eat all the cookies and ice cream they give you at their houses (because chances are you won't get as much at ours), and ask lots of questions. It's a special time in life. Enjoy every minute of it.

To Beverly: you opened the door and lit the way. I am one of thousands who walk this path, because of you.

Ya' know that old trees just grow stronger
And old rivers grow wilder every day
Old people just grow lonesome
Waiting for someone to say, "Hello in there, hello"

—John Prine, country-folk singer songwriter

CONTENTS

INTRODUCTION

On April 28, 2018, at 7:30 a.m., I experienced my greatest fear and my greatest blessing, and it all happened at once.

I went for a morning run with my sixteen-month-old daughter in our rough-and-tumble jogging stroller. We were running down a very quiet street in the Mar Vista neighborhood of Los Angeles. This is a safe and secure neighborhood, with young children playing in their front yards, and parents and grandparents walking with their morning coffee.

It was the perfect Southern California spring morning, with a slight chill in the air, and the warm sun rising. I had just removed my sweatshirt and placed it in the stroller. My daughter snacked on her favorite cereal.

As we were crossing the street on the corner of Navy and Inglewood, a grey car slowed down at the stop sign, but strangely kept rolling toward us. I hollered at the driver to get his attention. I was sure he would hear me and slow down. But the car kept coming, and then seemed to accelerate. I screamed in anger and then shock and then terror as the car slammed into the baby stroller with my daughter inside.

The stroller exploded out of my hands and went flying in the opposite direction.

Imagine my horror as I ran to the stroller which had collapsed on the ground, fifteen feet away from impact. My daughter was strapped into the stroller and crying hysterically. With my shaking hands, I unbuckled her and held her in my arms.

The driver sped away. It was a hit-and-run. It came out of nowhere. The firefighters arrived, then my wife and three-year-old son, then the police.

We took my daughter to the doctor and she was okay. I was okay. We dodged a bullet.

It all happened so fast, but in the moment before impact, I desperately tried to make eye contact with the driver. I could not see his eyes. He was looking down at what must have been his phone. As I write this, it is still an open investigation with the LAPD.

Whether or not they catch the driver, I am just grateful and fortunate to be able to share a happy ending to this story. But it was a warning to me, and to you. All a father wants to do is protect his children, and to think danger came exploding out of the blue on an otherwise tranquil weekend morning.

Now you might be thinking, *that's a scary story but what does this have to do with "the oldest and wisest"?*

Einstein said, "The distinction between the past, present, and future is only a stubbornly persistent illusion."

All of time is woven together and intricately connected, like one of those lanyards you create in 3rd grade. The past creates the future just as the future informs past. If I think too hard about it, I get confused.

But something happened in the days leading up to the hit-and-run incident with my daughter. I feel that I had been prepared for the meaning of the impact.

◆　◆　◆　◆

A few weeks prior to this hit-and-run incident, I received a rather blunt email from a woman named Tara. The message read, "Dave, I received your blog in the past and thought you were taking the branding kool-aid. So I never paid attention. But the work you are doing with elders is refreshing."

This one brief message sums up the arc of my personal journey. In the past, I combined yoga with chocolate and wine. It was all about *joie de vivre* and living in the moment. It was fun and playful, but it wasn't adding much value to the world.

Then I became a father and wanted to do something more meaningful. How could I, in some way, leave the world a better place than how I found it?

When my last surviving grandparent passed away in 2010, I realized it's hard to get old. But in America, we make it even harder. If it's not the aches and pains of aging, then it's the social isolation. Most elders do not have a prominent voice in our communities. Many are living lonely lives in retirement facilities, disconnected from the younger generations. And yet, these elders have so much history, so much to share.

So I put out a simple request to my community: "who is your favorite elder?"

Some people shared memories and inspirations from a favorite elder, many of which are included as little quips and quotes between the chapters to come.

Other people started connecting me with their grandmothers and elder mothers, college professors and high school art teachers, neighbors who are Holocaust survivors, nannies who have become mentors. They were all in their 80s, 90s, and 100s, and they all had something they wanted to share.

These elders told me many powerful life lessons that helped me become a more purposeful professional, a more vested parent, a more awakened husband.

Here's the thing. The advice from someone at the very end of their life is much different from someone in the middle of their life. An elder's wisdom is often raw, unscripted, unbranded, poignant, and deeply personal. It probably won't come to you in short, polished soundbites that you can cut and paste onto social media.

But I have found that if you ask an elder to share their story, and if you are willing to spend some time and listen to their answer, they will teach you something that you cannot learn from even the most successful self-help gurus or the most high-impact business coaches.

For example . . .

The aforementioned woman, Tara, responded to my request and invited me to Jackson, Mississippi, to meet some of her favorite elders. It's not exactly easy to get from Los Angeles to Jackson—with two small children at home, I find it hard enough to take a shower, let alone journey to the Deep South.

But the day after speaking to Tara, I was driving through Los Angeles and listening to the Grateful Dead Channel on Sirius. There was a concert playing in its entirety. For more than two hours, my car's radio display read:

Grateful Dead
Jackson, Mississippi
December 19, 1978

As Confucius said, "Signs and symbols rule the world. Not rules and laws."

Come April, I flew to New Orleans, rented a car, and took off on a gorgeous road trip up the I-55 to Mississippi. In April, the South is in full bloom with newly birthed bright green leaves, and purple, orange, and yellow wildflowers illuminating the entire interstate. Listening to a playlist with some Dierks Bentley and feeling momentarily free from the rigors of parenting, I sang, and at times *screamed*, "Free and easy down the road I go!"

Our first stop was a town outside of Jackson called Byram, Mississippi, population 11,489.

Tara took me to meet Eula, an African-American woman who was 105 years old, days away from turning 106. Eula and her niece answered the door to greet us. They led us past a spread of sandwiches and potato chips they had placed out for us, and into her living room.

I looked around at Eula's walls, decorated with 105 years of history. I saw a beautifully framed image that read "PRESIDENT OBAMA" from the night he was elected in 2008. Eula said the greatest moment of her life was "seeing a black man elected President."

I noticed a newspaper article about Eula's father, a World War I veteran, who died in 2000 at the age of 104.

Next to another Obama picture was a framed poster of Psalm 23:1-2, "The Lord is my Shepherd, I shall not want. He maketh me to lie down in green pastures; he leadeth me beside the still waters."

Eula wore a bright red sweater which matched a bright red pillow woven with a white cross lying just beside her. Painted portraits and photographs of her two children and late husband decorated the wall behind her.

The first thing she told me, proudly: "I live by myself."

Eula was born May 24, 1912, which made her seventeen years older than MLK and five years older than JFK.

I asked how old she feels on the inside.

She said in a deep Southern accent with a touch of gospel spirit, "I don't know how I feel on the inside or the outside. I just go."

Eula told us a little about her childhood. "We grew up on a white man's place down on the Pilgrim West Road. We had to walk to school three miles there and three miles back when we were just five years old. We had to walk in the rain and the mud, cold weather. School bus would run by and splash water up on us and children throwing spitballs out of the bus at us. But it didn't bother us. We just went right on. God is good."

Eula was one of nine siblings. She adopted two children, through whom she has thirteen grandchildren.

There is a lot of family and a lot of love in her life. Her niece, who greeted us, lives in the house across the road from Eula. She wakes up each morning, and looks across the road to make sure she sees Eula's little light on. She looks out for her, as do most of the people in their local church, many of whom are related to Eula. She is now the oldest person in the church, and her community looks to her for wisdom and advice.

Eula seems to be rounding the corner to 106 with her own kind of momentum. "I can't get around like I used to but I still enjoy waking up in the morning and seeing the sunshine. It's a joy to be livin'."

She has a great faith. "Do unto others as you would have others do unto you. And you'll be alright!" She asked for my favorite verse from the Bible and I responded, "I'm Jewish."

And she quipped, "Just cause you're Jewish don't keep you from havin' one."

She laughed out loud.

I looked around nervously to see if I said something I shouldn't have said. But Eula's laughter kept on going and kept on building. So I started laughing, hesitantly at first. But then the laughter caught on and my laugh is not exactly bashful. A 105-year-old Southern Baptist from Mississippi and a 45-year-old Jew from LA. "God is good!"

They say that laughter creates trust and what felt like a forced conversation began to find a little rhythm and flow.

I asked her if she believes in the afterlife. "It's there. Whether we get it or not, it's there. When the Lord says 'that's enough come on up, join the crowd,' I'm ready to go there."

She sang Amazing Grace for us. If only you could hear the spirit and history and antique beauty in her voice,

Amazing grace! how sweet the sound,
That saved a wretch like me!
I once was lost, but now am found,
Was blind, but now I see.

Her niece shared what may be Eula's special secret for longevity, aside from genetics: "She has seen her eight sisters go. And most of them she was very close to. The faith has sustained her. She is able to place [their loss], compartmentalize it, and keep goin'."

That is the part which really stayed with me. "Compartmentalize."

As part of my work in life, I teach mindfulness. When you are mindful, you gain control of your attention. If you are stuck thinking of something that makes you unhappy, you have the power to extricate your attention and place it on something productive, positive, peaceful.

That's the same message I heard from Eula's niece—compartmentalize.

After that hit-and-run incident with my daughter, so many people kept running through how much worse it could have been. "What if she wasn't strapped in!" or "What if the car hit you?" or "What if the stroller didn't land on its back?"

I kept thinking and hearing that word from Eula's niece. Compartmentalize.

Seeing your own child struck by a car in front of your own eyes has the potential to make you feel helpless and endangered.

I had to move forward and put this incident in a place where I could make use of it. I needed to compartmentalize it.

But there was another message I received in Mississippi which showed me the path forward.

◆ ◆ ◆ ◆

The next day, Tara and I drove to Shubuta, Mississippi, population 441. Surely you've heard of Shubuta? Small town two hours east of Jackson close to the border with Alabama?

Tara's Aunt Patsy, 89, met us at the church. She held four American flags and a handwritten sign "Welcome Tara and David."

Southern hospitality right from the get-go!

I live in Los Angeles. When you have a guest in LA, you tell them to Uber to your home and you'll see them later.

Not only did Patsy meet us upon arrival, she took us straight to her favorite rib shack in rural Mississippi. This rib shack was surrounded by, not Starbucks and Rite Aids, but pine trees in every direction.

Patsy knew everyone in the rib shack from the local garbageman who thanked her for the t-shirt she recently gifted him, to the lady who owned the rib shack and commented when Patsy dropped her keys and quickly bent down to pick them up without even thinking of asking for help.

We left the rib shack with a bag of burgers and fries which Patsy dropped off for a man in a pickup truck down the road. Patsy then gave us a tour of Shubuta. She showed us the old jail cell, the cemetery, the deer hunting lodge. She led us on a ride down the main strip past a sign that said "Drive-by Prayer."

I should note there was a gun in her car, right next to my feet.

"Is this loaded?" I asked, my voice cracking.

"It's a BB gun, dear. I've never used it," she answered.

I asked Patsy how she maintains her social vitality.

"Use your skills," she told me.

"What's your skill?" I inquired.

"I'm a good listener. You don't learn anything talkin'. You only learn listenin'."

Personally, I'm a good talker, not as good of a listener. Over the course of fourteen years, I have built a platform via email and social media through which I've done a lot of talking and writing about living in the moment, spreading the love, being mindful of our elders.

But in the days following the hit-and-run incident with my daughter, I kept listening and hearing those words from Patsy, in her Mississippi drawl, "Use your skills."

So I leaned in and used my platform on email and social media to spread the message about what went down with my daughter and the strong possibility that the driver was distracted. "Think carefully about reaching for your phone while you're in a 4,000 pound machine going 20, 30, even 10 mph."

And yet almost everyone is a distracted driver, myself included.

The policeman at the scene of the hit-and-run told us that distracted driving is the single most common ticket he writes. And the person receiving the ticket almost always complains that it was absolutely crucial to send the text message and there's no way they should get that ticket. "It's not fair!"

Try telling that to a parent whose stroller you "accidentally" collided with while you just had to send that text message.

I shared the story of what happened to my daughter on every possible social media channel, via my podcast and blog, on every call with every friend, with every Uber driver I rode with.

Countless people commented and shared their own story of being the victim of a distracted driver. One lady, Dora, shared how she was walking on a crosswalk across Montana Avenue in Santa Monica. This is one of the most upscale streets in the most upscale beach town. And a minivan with a distracted driver slammed into her, rendering her unconscious and hospitalized. She had three fractures in her pelvis and sacrum.

Another woman, Wendy, told me, "My daughter and I were walking in the parking lot in her school. A car that was backing up hit us and knocked us to the ground partially dragging my daughter underneath the car. The car seemed to be accelerating but I think my daughter's piercing screams caught the driver's attention. It was horrifying."

My sharing this story stirred up a powerful conversation and many people, like me, admitted their guilt as distracted drivers and promised to stop looking at their phone in the car.

In moments when I start reliving those horrifying moments when the stroller was hit and my daughter's fate was unknown, I remind myself:

"Compartmentalize." I put the incident to use as a motivator, as fuel for my fire.

"Use Your Skills." I now understand I have an audience for this very reason: to change the life of even just one reader who might hear my story, put their phone down while driving, and actually see the baby stroller, or the old man, or the mom walking across the street with her children.

I believe those messages prepared me for that harrowing moment to come just a few days later. I continue to hear those words delivered in that Mississippi drawl, over and over and over. "Compartmentalize," "use your skills," "compartmentalize," "use your skills."

That is the inspiration behind this book. To remind you, or awaken you, to the wisdom of your elders and how it can be a missing ingredient that helps you make sense of all your thoughts and challenges and questions. This elder wisdom is healing medicine made with 80, 90, 100 years of history, pain, and love. But the only way this medicine works is if you take it.

In the pages to come, I will share how the elder wisdom has the potential to improve your relationships with your partner and your children. Some of the elders I interviewed raised five or seven or nine children, as single moms. They know a thing or two about parenting.

Other elders managed to survive the Nazis and Auschwitz or five months as a POW. They know a thing or two about getting through hard times.

And others have a great sense of humor and will remind you to keep it light and easy when you tend to make it dark and difficult.

Of course these elders should have a prominent voice and place in our communities. Right?

◆　◆　◆　◆

Most younger people don't look to older people for wisdom. By "younger," I mean people ages 15-55 years old, who may or may not have a grandparent and in many cases do not have a single elder in their social circles.

Instead, many younger people get their wisdom from a 29-year-old yoga "guru" with a massive following on Instagram who quotes Rumi from their epic handstand on a beach in Bali. Or you might get your wisdom from a well-educated therapist who gives very helpful advice on marriage and sex and addiction. Or your advice might come from a *New York Times* bestselling author who is super talented and does tons of research and writes beautiful prose, cited by none other than Oprah.

And trust me, I'm a consumer. I look to Instagram for a quick quote, and I've been to therapy, and I read the bestselling self-help books, and I love SuperSoulSunday.

But what about the elders?! Many of these people in their 80s and 90s and 100s endured the Great Depression, fought in World War II, survived the Holocaust, marched for civil rights, watched (in Eula's case) nineteen presidencies, and bounced back from (in Eula's case) nineteen economic recessions. They've been through so much and would love to share their wisdom.

So why aren't old people giving more advice to young people?

1. Many elders are isolated. If you can't drive, it's hard to get around. I overheard a 93-year-old woman complaining that her children recently took away her car. They feared that with her failing eyesight, she was a hazard on the roads. So you are not likely to stumble across too many elders in the flow of your everyday life, at the office, waiting for your yoga class to begin, or picking up the kids from school.

2. Even if an elder can drive, old age can be painful and exhausting. It's more likely that someone in their very old age will spend most of their time alone at home or in a retirement community.

So that leaves us with a major disconnect in our communities. The elder knowledge and wisdom is a profoundly precious resource. And many of these elders are isolated, lonely, and segregated by age. We can do better and we have to do better.

In the pages to come, I will introduce you to twenty elders, all of whose stories and lessons have the potential to impact "young people" doing their best to figure out how to balance marriage and parenting, or work and life, or grief and growth. It's tough out there, and most everyone I know is struggling to find balance.

I hope these stories will inspire you to seek out and meet the elders on your street, in your neighborhood, in your community. Or maybe there is an elder who you already have access to, a grandparent or relative, who you take for granted. Their time is limited. Don't put this off.

Only 558,000 of the 16 million Americans who served in World War II were alive in 2017.

An average of 372 of these surviving WWII veterans are dying each day.

It's one thing to read about Pearl Harbor, but it's entirely different to hear the story firsthand of the black smoke rising around the USS Arizona on the morning of December 7, 1941.

There are only 100,000 Holocaust survivors alive in 2018, and more than 1,000 pass away each month.

In ten years, most, if not all Holocaust survivors will be gone.

There are countless movies and documentaries about the Holocaust. But it's not the same as hearing an Auschwitz survivor describe the pain of watching her mother and four siblings dragged into the gas chamber. (See Chapter 3.)

Life is precious. Most World War II veterans and Holocaust survivors will probably tell you they are lucky to be alive. I was reminded of this message when my daughter's stroller was hit by a car. You just never know. How many times have you heard the message to make every day count?

For someone who is 105, or 99, or 92, it's not just about making every day count. Any breath could be their last.

Before it's too late, these are my questions:

What do you have to share with us?

What is your advice to young people on how to live a good life?

What are your regrets?

What are your secrets to health?

How do you find your way in the darkness?

How do you make sense of the madness?

Enough with all the questions.

Now let's hear the answers.

1

OVERCOME THE GRIND

I've never had bullets fly by my head. But I've experienced freedom because of men who did. Forever thankful for every veteran's sacrifice.

—Anonymous

I live in Los Angeles, where the grind means driving in traffic.

Any Los Angeleno will tell you to avoid the roads from 6:00 a.m. to 9:00 a.m., and 4:00 p.m. to 7:00 p.m. And if you tell a local you are about to drive the freeway at the wrong time of day, it's like telling them you have a bad case of syphilis.

Every time I enter my destination on Google Maps, it says it will take fifty-seven minutes to go 4.3 miles through Los Angeles gridlock.

I'll begin those fifty-seven minutes to get 4.3 miles by making calls to friends or relatives. Mom, dad, brother, friends from high school, friends from college, maybe a new friend, although those are harder to make at this stage in life. I'd like to make some new friends. Why don't I have any new friends? Maybe because I'm spending too much time in this traffic!

Then I'll put on the Grateful Dead Channel on Sirius. The sparkles from Jerry Garcia's guitar always relax my mind and remind me of a time in the early 90s when the only worry I had in the world was if I had tickets to the next Dead show. Sometimes there will be a song on the Grateful Dead Channel from a show I actually attended, Cal Expo in '92, Shoreline in '93, Atlanta in '94. Then they will play a song with a jam that's a little too long and I'll remember how much time I'm actually spending in traffic!

After the Dead, I'll switch to Anne Lamott or Marianne Williamson on Audible. Lamott makes me laugh. I marvel at her prowess as a writer, balancing God and Jesus and still managing to drop those F-bombs with grace and style. And Williamson reminds me that the Holy Spirit is alive and well! But then, I'll ask myself, where is the Holy Spirit to help me with this traffic?!

And there are still thirty-two minutes left to get 2.7 miles. God and Jesus help me!

I teach happiness and mindfulness. But this traffic is a catalyst for absolute *insanity*.

Almost every day, while bemoaning my bumper-to-bumper fate, I'll pass by the Los Angeles National Cemetery on Sepulveda Boulevard. It's a massive cemetery which I've been driving past for thirty years. I never once even considered stopping to pay my respects.

That is, until I received an email from someone who had taken one of my yoga workshops in New York City. Julie wrote, "I would like to introduce you to my wonderful parents

Joseph and Joan. Together in love still after over sixty-two years of marriage. My dad served in the Korean War and is a decorated veteran. He still to this day serves as a volunteer assisting with prayers and ceremonies for those veterans who have perished. They attend mass on a regular basis, lead a life of dignity and service, and are a constant pillar of strength for each one of us."

Amen!

Her father, Joe, was just a kid in his early twenties, fighting on the front line in Korea, in a war where 36,000 young Americans lost their lives.

Joe explained, "During war, you are not thinking in social terms, you're just trying to stay alive."

At a young age when I was smoking pot, going to Grateful Dead concerts, watching Lakers and 49ers games, and feeling absolutely no urgency, Joe was fighting at the 38th parallel.

He glossed over the bloody details of war. But I did prod once and Joe shared a particularly gruesome story of Turkish soldiers displaying the body parts of their fallen enemy as a sort of decoration or medal.

Let it be clear, Joe didn't send me down this line of thinking. He repeatedly told me how lucky he has been, all his life. He just wanted to talk about his amazing wife who always has a smile and the love he has for his family of thirty-two—including seven children, fifteen grandchildren, and three great-grandchildren.

Joe shared with me his path out of Korea and into his civilian life as a quality control expert.

Now 86 years old, Joe described how his fierce love for country inspires his ongoing service as a chaplain at a veterans hospital, along with his involvement in associations like Disabled American Veterans, American Legion, Veterans of Foreign Wars, and Korean War Veterans.

And he failed to mention that he just happened to be awarded a Bronze Star, a Combat Infantry Badge, a Korean Service Medal, a UN Medal, a Defense Medal, and a few others he didn't recall off the top of his head. His daughter just mentioned he was "decorated." I had to ask Joe for the details.

A few days after speaking with Joe, I again sat in traffic on Sepulveda Boulevard, right there alongside the Los Angeles National Cemetery. But this time, instead of sitting in gridlock, I pulled into the parking lot of the cemetery to explore.

Some 88,000 American veterans are buried there.

I picked up a map which highlighted the graves of Medal of Honor recipients buried at the Los Angeles National Cemetery. I felt a calling to visit the grave of one Charles W. Rundle, a Union Army soldier and recipient of the Medal of Honor, for his actions during the Siege of Vicksburg in the Civil War.

He was 21 years old on May 22, 1863, when Union commanders called for 150 unmarried volunteers to charge a heavily fortified Confederate position; Rundle answered the call.

As Rundle and the others ran across the open ground in front of the fort, Confederate cannons opened fire and inflicted heavy casualties. Only 30 of the original 150 men made it back. Rundle receive the Medal of Honor for gallantry in the charge of the "volunteer storming party."

Rundle spent his later years in Santa Monica, California, and was buried in the Los Angeles National Cemetery upon his death in 1924.

Over 41,000,000 Americans have served the military during wartime. Only 3,517 Americans have received the Medal of Honor.

I was honored to spend a morning, two miles from my home, standing at the resting place of one such recipient. He was just a 21-year-old kid storming the Confederates just as Joe was 21 and fighting on the front line in Korea.

I'm guessing Joe and Charles W. Rundle did not complain much about anything, let alone traffic.

Joe's daughter confirmed this: "Dad raised me and six other siblings and sent us all to college. He worked the late shift every night, got home at 4:00 a.m., never complained, and never missed a day of work."

That statement really awakened me. He "never complained." After battling in a war and raising seven kids and putting them all through college and working the late shift for decades... and he never complained!

To think how much I complain about, outwardly, inwardly, to my partner, to my God, to anyone who will listen.

Just yesterday, I was driving in Friday traffic to the pharmacy to get a prescription. Bumper to bumper. I started to slip into a state of woe, and remembered I had a choice. I always have a choice.

After the Korean War, Joe chose a life and attitude of strength. He said, "If you don't know what you want, people will walk all over you."

Thank you, Joe. Let me tell you what I want.

When I'm at a standstill on Santa Monica Boulevard, I want to remember Joe and Charles W. Rundle. They were kids fighting for our freedom and didn't complain about it.

Do I have any right to complain when it's taking me five extra minutes to get to CVS for my Charmin Ultra Soft and Z-pac?

I want to poke my head through the fog and feel grateful for all the freedoms that I enjoy. Despite the traffic, I can get in my car and go anywhere right now. I can say anything about anyone anytime. I can start any business my heart desires. In places like Russia or North Korea or China, those freedoms don't exist. I am a spoiled brat about my overabundance of freedom, the great American luxury fought for and won by Joe and by Charles W. Rundle.

I want to change my attitude and choose "a life of strength," when the kids are screaming, when business is ebbing more than flowing, when I am stuck on the dark side of a moody Monday.

That shift in attitude might not affect the gridlock on the roads and highways, but it can and it will free the gridlock in the mind. Release the thoughts which lock you up and hold you down. Make space for the thoughts that pick you up and set you free.

That's where the grind comes to an end, and the flow begins.

"My great-aunt Elberta died at 101. She rarely complained and said she'd regret spending the time complaining takes, when she could just as easily find something to enjoy."

—Sandy, Godfrey, Illinois

2

FEEL YOUNG FOREVER

Said the little boy, "Sometimes I drop my spoon."
Said the old man, "I do that too."
The little boy whispered, "I wet my pants."
"I do that too," laughed the little old man.
Said the little boy, "I often cry."
The old man nodded, "So do I."
"But worst of all," said the boy, "it seems
Grown-ups don't pay attention to me."
And he felt the warmth of a wrinkled old hand.
"I know what you mean," said the little old man.
                                    —Shel Silverstein

Grandparents.

Is there anything better?

They spoil you. They cherish you. They let you break the rules.

You energize them. You appreciate them. You let *them* break the rules.

When I was young, I would get so excited for my grandparents to visit from the East Coast. My Grandpa Joe and I played catch for hours. He came to my Little League and high school baseball games. My Grandma Evelyn loved flowers and painting and everything felt more beautiful when she was around. My Grandpa Bert made the most delicious Italian food (gnocchi and risotto and string beans slathered in vinegar and butter) and my Grandma Neda, with her strong Italian accent, embodied resilience and confidence and gave me the most sage advice ever: "Stop using all that hairspray!"

Your grandparents get old and older and really old. And they die. It's over. Just like that. No more grandparents.

Most of my friends and colleagues, in their 40s, do not have a single elder in their life. And that's fine. You can live without an elder. It probably won't affect your business or your health.

But are we missing something when we stop communicating with an entire generation? My answer is a resounding *yes!*

In 2017, I began a series of events called Drinks with Your Elders. At independent book stores in five cities around the USA, I invited fascinating elders in their 80s and 90s to come and share their stories with younger people.

I invited friends and followers on social media. I texted, emailed, and made videos. "Come have Drinks with Your Elders: Friday at 7pm. Cost: FREE!"

One person replied to my invite, "I don't understand. You want me to come talk to old people?"

I answered, "There will be wine at the event. Plus, people in their 80s and 90s have some really awesome stories."

"Okay. It's on my radar."

I pushed a little more, "The wine is free."

"Free wine? Fine. I'll stop by for a few minutes."

Convincing the elders to attend was a whole other conversation.

"Nobody wants to hear what I have to say," responded one 88-year-old lady on the phone who I invited to come and speak at the Drinks with Your Elders event in Chicago.

I told her, "Your story is so powerful. Young people need to hear from you."

"I don't have a way to get there," she answered.

"I'll pick you up. I'll make it easy for you."

"No. It's too late for me. I get tired at the end of the day."

It's easy to see why our society is segregated by age. We go to our separate corners, on our phones, in our homes, in front of our TVs. If we go out and socialize, it's usually with people around our same age.

This "Drinks with Your Elders" thing was going to take more work than I originally thought. I needed to find some *renegade* elders, willing to do something totally different.

Phoenix, Arizona, was the first stop on the Drinks with Your Elders Tour. The day of the event, we had "drinks" but we didn't have any "elders." A friend introduced me to Bernie, 100 years old, who she knew from her "shul" or synagogue.

This synagogue has a preschool and Bernie asked me to meet him on the playground. We were surrounded by the sound and energy of twenty or more young children ages 3 to 8 years old. They were playing on the slide and the swings and the seesaw.

Sometimes you meet a 100-year-old, and they are every bit of 100, huffing and puffing to get from one moment to the next. But the second I heard Bernie's laugh, I felt something timeless, silly, and deeply integrated with the energy of all these squawking, crying, laughing, playful children surrounding us.

Bernie agreed to be the featured elder at that night's Drinks with Your Elders event.

He drove himself to the event at the Changing Hands Bookstore. He stood up to address the crowd and share his story.

His family emigrated from Russia in 1921, and ended up in Harrisburg, Pennsylvania. He instantly captured everyone's attention when he told us a story from the days of Prohibition.

People would come into his family's grocery store and buy 100-pound bags of sugar. Only four years old at the time, Bernie was curious and asked what one such customer was doing with all this sugar. They invited cute little Bernie upstairs to a secret room with barrels and barrels of mash, or sugar-based moonshine, the form of alcohol commonly consumed in the years of the Prohibition from 1920-1933.

One day, Prohibitions agents came, found the barrels, rolled them down onto the street, and took hatchets to the barrels. Bernie recalled how the moonshine was flooding out of the barrels and down the curb, forming a creek. People ran over with cups to get what they could. He said, "It was just like an Al Capone movie!"

I don't think anyone in the audience had ever heard a firsthand account of the Prohibition. We were hooked on Bernie. And he was hooked on us! After the event, a revitalized Bernie hammed it up with the crowd, who felt enlightened by these stories from a distant past.

I wanted to know more. How does a 100-year-old man have so much vigor? I stayed in touch with Bernie and over a year later, we reconnected.

In 1934, Bernie and his family moved from Pennsylvania to Phoenix, where he still lives today. He resides alone, in the same GI-bill house he moved into immediately after World War II.

Bernie has lost all of his siblings and his wife. He stays busy by visiting his synagogue three times each week. In describing his routine, he constantly asked me questions and kept me on my toes.

"When I go to the shul, they have what you call on Saturday a Chumash. Do you know what a Chumash is?"

I answered, "No."

"Do you know what a Parsha is?"

"No."

"No, you don't," he quipped. "It's a section in the Torah they read every Saturday from the Five Books of Moses. Every Saturday they go to the next Parsha or section. To me it's historical. Do you understand?"

"Yes. Sort of."

I was supposed to be the one asking Bernie questions. And in this particular follow-up conversation, I wanted to get a quote or message from Bernie, something I could easily share in this book.

But Bernie took it so much deeper than that.

At the time, he was honoring a holiday called Shavuot, which recognizes when Moses climbed Mount Sinai and received the Ten Commandments directly from God.

"Moses talked to God. Did you know that?" he asked me.

"A little bit."

He continued, "You knew that?! Not many people know that."

I mean, I barely knew that, to be honest with you. I never understood the significance of Moses receiving the commandments. I thought it was Hebrew school mumbo jumbo. But all that was about to change.

Bernie emphasized, "Not many people speak to God person to person!"

Bernie inspired me to study up on Shavuot.

Our connection with God is only as deep as our current understanding. We all have limitations. Consider a light bulb. If you run too much voltage through a light bulb, it will burn out or worse, explode.

How do you increase the voltage? How do you increase your capacity to carry more love and more wisdom and more abundance? How do you expand from your level of understanding to God's all-encompassing level of understanding?

I reached out to one of my very wise, spiritual friends. "Did you know that today is Shavuot? Do you know what that is?"

He replied, "I just had a cold plunge and sat around the biocharger with my Rabbi. We talked about Shavuot. It's a powerful day."

I'm not sure what a biocharger is. But he confirmed my belief that this Shavuot is a bigger deal than I ever imagined it to be.

"It means getting your inspiration straight from God, right?"

My friend confirmed, "Direct download from Source."

I thought back to the unique setting in which I met Bernie. He was surrounded by children on the playground. I had been distracted by all these kids, and I was struggling to concentrate. But now I get it. There is something about the energy of very young children. It is the most loving energy in the universe.

As I write this, I have a nineteen-month-old daughter and a three-year-old son at home. When I look at pictures from this stage in my life, I always look tired. But I am always smiling. Children ignite a certain kind of joy.

Once the kids grow up, we lose direct access to this kind of joy. Maybe you don't want access. You've been there, done that.

But therein lies the disconnect between generations.

Why don't the very old spend more time with the very young?

I spoke to a woman in Atlanta whose children attend a preschool connected with a senior living center. She said, "The school supports the elders throughout the year. The kindergarten class has the closest relationship. They make Derby hats with the elders. They put on performances for them. They bring them cards and art projects for the holidays. The Halloween parade goes through the senior living center and the kids talk about their costume inspirations with the elders.

"Many of the elders there don't have family, or don't leave the facility, so the main benefit is companionship. The elders really love it.

"As for the children, the main purpose is to teach them kindness, empathy, but also exposing them to different generations. It's such a rich learning experience."

Bernie ascribes to this same kind of intergenerational magic. Every Saturday, he goes to his synagogue and the kids gather round on the playground as he gives them fruit roll-ups. The kids know his name, and he knows their names.

He said the kids make him feel "beautiful, wonderful."

Bernie goes straight to the source and gets a direct download of childlike joy and youthful spunk. The kids get an extra grandparent to spoil them with fruit roll-ups.

Moderation need not apply. An elder can never have too much youth. And a youth can never have too many grandparents.

"My grandmother, Dottie, was vibrant and full of life. We were all attracted by her zest, her sense of humor, and her ability to easily be the life of the party. I will always remember the purple hair she had when she was older—she swears Clairol changed the formula and she didn't do anything differently. Her Creme de Menthe Grasshopper Pie (which made me sick at a family party when I innocently ingested most of it, not realizing it contained alcohol); and how she tore her meniscus in her knee when she performed the chicken dance too aggressively at the annual German Oktoberfest in our hometown. I can never hear that song without smiling!"

—Julie, Newport Beach, California

3

HOW TO HEAL YOUR RELATIONSHIPS

We can only be said to be alive in those moments when our hearts are conscious of our treasures.
—Thornton Wilder, American playwright

What does it take for you to have a really great day? Does it mean taking a sweaty hot yoga class with awesome music and feeling super relaxed and detoxified? Is it about time in the warm sunshine, your worries melting away? Maybe a glass of red wine and a good book?

For me, there was a three-month window where the only thing that constituted "a great day" was lifting my 5'10" Jewish Dad-bod with man-boobs and jumping HIGH off the ground to slam-dunk a basketball on a ten-foot rim!

Let me explain.

In 2016, I met an athletic trainer, Matt, who works with professional athletes. Most of his clients play professional baseball, football, hockey, and basketball.

Matt, only 5'6", can dunk a basketball on a ten-foot rim.

"Okay, dude," I had to ask. "If I trained with you every day, could you teach me how to dunk?"

He was intrigued.

We put together the Slam Dunk Challenge and invited people to pledge their support (and money). I trained with Matt every day for three months to dunk it home. All proceeds went to the Wounded Warrior Project.

Each and every day, I trained with Matt to increase my vertical leap, strength, and speed.

It was quite the juxtaposition to see me, white and hairy and "not exactly svelte," as one former girlfriend told me, training next to pitchers for the Braves, White Sox, and Cardinals who throw 100-mph fastballs, and linebackers for the Vikings, Falcons, and Raiders who run 4.3-second forty-yard dashes.

Throughout these three months, I would send my friends photos and videos of my increasing vertical leap, and say things like "Look how high I get in this picture!" One friend replied, "I'd rather you send me pictures of your kids."

It was then I realized that my bright white legs jumping a few inches off the ground to touch the air conditioning pipes on the ceiling in Matt's gym were not exactly Michael Jordan soaring to the rim.

Nonetheless, I trained hard and believed I would at least be able to touch the rim and defy my doubters while inspiring my supporters.

Day after day, Matt slipped me into his busy training schedule, between his appointments with elite athletes wondering what the hell I was doing there. I stood out like a sore thumb—"sore" being the key word, as many days I could not walk up the stairs in my home. My lats and quads and triceps and biceps were twitching and burning, at their absolute maximum threshold.

The big day came. I stretched and warmed up at a friend's house with a regulation basketball hoop and breakaway rim. A crowd gathered. Matt was there to show his support.

I laced up my shoes, dribbled the ball, began my approach, picked up speed, angled toward the hoop, bent my knees low, and *jumped* as high as I possibly could!

The people gasped in awe, their mouths hung open, watching as I rose off the ground, my feet soaring above the ants and spiders, lifting higher and higher, centimeters became inches, inches turned into . . .

Thud!

I only touched the backboard and landed on the ground with a "plop."

Friend after friend called and asked, "So did you dunk it?"

"I added six inches to my vertical leap and touched where the rim hits the backboard!"

"Wait, what? Did you dunk it?"

"We raised more than $3,000 for the Wounded Warrior Project."

"Answer the question!"

"I'm still working on it. My trainer said if I train for three more months, I could do it!"

I didn't have the heart to tell them that I didn't dunk it. And it's true. Matt said I just needed more time to train. But then my second child was born and with two kids in diapers, time became the most precious and rarest thing in the world.

How do you possibly balance staying in shape, being a nurturing parent, building your career, having a good marriage, maintaining friendships, working on your house, getting your car washed, cleaning out the desk drawers, shaving your beard, and fixing the fire alarm that needs to be replaced, and by the way . . . I have no clue how I finished this book but if you're reading it right now, let it be known there is a God and there are miracles!

How do you do it all?!

◆ ◆ ◆ ◆

Blanca wrote to me, "My mom is the most positive person in the world. I know because in fifty-three years of my life she has never gotten mad at me or my sisters. I have never seen her upset or down—she is always happy with a big smile and very sweet. Full of proverbs and old wives' tales! People love her. I think she is a magnet!"

Through her daughter translating from Spanish, Antonia told about her life of humble beginnings growing up in Mexico. She always received a great love from her mom. She remembered her mom waiting for her after school, with something to share: a hug, or delicious corn bread made on the wood-fired stove in their kitchen. She recalled how her mom would braid her hair and show love in the ways she was able to show love.

The Italian priest and scholar Giovanni Giocondo said, "No heaven can come to us unless our hearts find rest in it today. Take heaven. No peace lies in the future which is not hidden in this present little instant. Take peace."

On that note, no love can be felt unless we experience it this very moment. Take love and give love in any way you can . . . right now.

Antonia passed this "great love" on to her daughter Blanca, who always knew her mother would be waiting for her after school and they'd go home to something simmering in the kitchen.

"She would cook us mole, caldo de pollo, frijoles a la charra, nopalitos, and spaghetti with cheese, olive oil, butter, and parsley."

But the greatest memory, which brought tears to Blanca's eyes: "When we walked in the room, my mother dropped everything. She always concentrated on you. 'How are you? Are you hungry?' She acknowledged you."

To actually look at someone when they enter the room? That means looking away from the post that just popped up on your Instagram feed. That means looking away from the latest highlight on Sportscenter or the dramatic moment on your favorite Bravo show. That means looking away from any kind of tablet, iPhone, TV, or tech gizmo and actually looking in the eyes of this other person who just walked into the room.

Speaking of Instagram, one day I posted an image of Antonia and the story of looking someone in the eyes when they enter the room. My wife saw it and was touched by it. She walked into my home office to talk about it, and I waved her off because I only had a few minutes to get my work done before the kids woke up from their nap. What happened to looking her in the eyes?

Forget trying to get my dad-bod off the ground and toward the rim. The real athleticism is leaving your work behind and showing up for the ones you love, day after day, night after night. It is an athleticism of the mind and heart, and it's hard to do.

Blanca said, "My mother always makes you feel like you are the most important person."

Is that not an attainable goal, right now? Next time you share a moment with someone you care about, can you make them feel like you see them, like you love them, like you want nothing more than to share the moment you're in? I'm asking the question because I failed this test the moment after I wrote about it. Maybe you can do better?

St. Augustine said, "You have to start your relationship with God all over from the beginning every day."

You can always start fresh with the next chance you get. It doesn't necessarily mean it will be a "slam dunk." God knows I've been rejected by the rim, or worse, the backboard. Relationships aren't healed in seconds. Tech addiction doesn't just go away. But you can make the effort. A really good effort. Your very best effort. The most amazing effort you've made in years!

As Antonia said, "No one is perfect. Just try to become better each day."

"Ramona Hope, 88, was my dad's big sister. My husband described her as a living saint. She never had children but had a passion for her nieces and nephews and her whole family. She gave us every moment we needed and more. We all craved her love and attention, and it was always abundantly enough. She taught us to love those you're graced with in your life and give yourself to them and love will sustain all."

—Mike, Plano, Texas

4

FOR THE "JUDGY" ONES (yeah, you)

The ability to observe without evaluating is the highest form of intelligence.

—Krishnamurti, Indian philosopher

I judge people all the time.

Don't pretend like you're innocent. C'mon. We all get a little "judgy" sometimes.

I took my son to this celebrity book reading in LA. Actress Kristen Bell was reading to a room full of little kids. My son called her "the teacher," not knowing she was the voice of Anna in *Frozen*, not to mention the star of *Forgetting Sarah Marshall*, *Veronica Mars*, and a lot other movies and TV shows.

The moms and a few dads stood on the perimeter of the room watching Kristen Bell read to their children. It might just be me, but I'm pretty sure many of the parents, myself included, were judging Kristen Bell. How could you not? She puts herself out there as a major star. Of course we are going to judge her.

I thought to myself, *Why does she have to be so dramatic while reading this silly kids' book? She's kind of annoying. She sure is pretty, though . . . but annoying . . . but pretty.*

I studied the other parents. They were looking her up and down—her shoes, her pants, her blouse, her voice, her skin.

If you judge people, does it mean you are a bad person? I think judging is less about good and bad and more a sign of distraction and seduction, an inability to harness your mind, of which I am often guilty.

Can you quiet your mind and lead with your heart? If you're going to judge, can you explore someone's spirit and energy as much as their skin and style?

◆ ◆ ◆ ◆

A local Austinite took me to meet her friend Ina, who just turned 94.

Ina has lived in the same house for ninety years. Her house is surrounded by bars and restaurants on what has become a main boulevard in Austin. The city has grown up around her.

But Ina refuses to budge. She was there first! She had told my friend about a time when the mailman came on a horse and buggy. Now cars are whizzing past her front porch, which she was out sweeping when I met her.

Ina was hunched over. I couldn't really understand what she was saying. The whole thing made me sad.

And then I started judging her and thinking to myself:

I can't believe she still lives in this house alone.
She needs someone to take care of her.

*How is it possible she still drives when she struggles
to stand up straight?*

Shame on me.

I am trying to start a conversation about doing better for
our elders, and here I was breaking this old lady down from
head to toe. But then, this 94-year-old led us to her backyard,
which is one of the most dazzling and surprising moments
I've had in many, many years. Her backyard is a masterpiece
of landscaping and natural beauty. I followed her along a
winding path past blossoming trees and flowers and beautifully landscaped nooks and crannies.

Mind you, this 94-year old, hunched over, sounding as if
she was talking gibberish, tends to this massive garden all by
herself.

I had totally judged (and misjudged) Ina and realized
how naive I am about life and nature and the language of
spirit. I wanted a message, a quote, a cute little story from
this woman. And then I realized, something different was
taking shape.

"Words" don't tend a garden, nor a body, nor the world.

Anne Lamott said, "The thing about *light* is that it really
isn't yours, it's what you gather and shine back. And it gets
more power from reflectiveness; if you sit still and take it in, it
fills your cup, and then you can give it off yourself."

Love and light. Love and light. Love and light.

It's a powerful mantra, but only when you give it power.

In my twenties, I read the famous book "Autobiography
of a Yogi," in which Paramahansa Yogananda describes the
magic of the botanist and plant expert Luther Burbank.

Yogananda shared a conversation with Burbank:

"While I was conducting experiments to make 'spineless' cacti," Burbank said, "I often talked to the plants to create a vibration of love. 'You have nothing to fear,' I would tell them. 'You don't need your defensive thorns. I will protect you.' Gradually the useful plant of the desert emerged in a thornless variety."

Just to make that clear. This dude talked a cactus out of growing thorns.

Luther Burbank was a star in his day (1849-1926), visited by everyone from the King and Queen of Belgium to Jack London; from Grover Cleveland to John Muir.

There is something wild and free about one who knows the laws of nature. Here are a few of them:

1. THERE ARE NO STRAIGHT LINES IN NATURE

We want our lives to evolve on a certain path, forward and upward, and keep going and don't stop! And yet, if you look at nature, you will not find a straight line.

Your life may not evolve exactly as you expect or hope. You can keep fighting that battle. Or you can find peace and freedom in your winding and weaving path.

French writer Rene Crevel said, "The song of the curved line is called happiness."

In my conversations with elders, I try to ask questions in a chronological order. But their memories often come in flashes, not drawn-out chronological sequences.

Mario, 75, spoke at the Drinks with Your Elders event in New York City. He just randomly began telling me about his cousin who was a struggling actor and never got accepted into the Yale Repertory Theatre School. I had no clue where this came from and where he was going with it.

He described how his cousin got a job waiting tables at an upscale Chinese restaurant in New York City. One day, Steven Spielberg ate lunch with his mom and several others at this restaurant.

Spielberg's mom was charmed by Mario's cousin and kept going to the restaurant and sitting at his table. She asked him, "What is it you do outside of the restaurant?"

He said, "I'm an actor."

She responded, "My son is Spielberg."

A few months later, Mario's cousin had a full scholarship to UCLA's drama school graduate program.

You just never know what's around the corner on this winding and weaving path through life.

2. NATURE MOVES SLOWLY, BUT SURELY

There's a redwood that is 2,000 years old, a bristlecone pine tree that is 4,800 years old, and a Norway spruce that's 9,500 years old. They grow slowly . . . but surely.

There is a time-lapse video of a morning glory vine. The plant is rotating like a radar dish, searching and feeling around for a suitable support on which to grow. It is very much a living being. Your naked eye would struggle to notice this movement, as it is sped up through time-lapse video.

What else might our naked eye be missing because we move at such a frenzied pace? Might our need for speed be the seductive poison that only can be healed by a sometimes bitter dose of slowness?

Most elders, by natural process, move and talk more slowly than a young person is accustomed to. But who is really out of sync? The slow-talking elder with her eyes on the trees or the fast-talking youth with his eyes on a tiny, blinking screen?

3. NATURE IS THE BEST TEACHER

The average human spends ten hours a day in front of a screen. You can learn so much from the Internet. But is it the same as putting your feet on the grass, your hands on the trees, and your eyes to the skies?

As Luther Burbank said, "Every child should have mud pies, grasshoppers, water bugs, tadpoles, frogs, mud turtles, elderberries, wild strawberries, acorns, chestnuts, trees to climb, brooks to wade, water lilies, woodchucks, bats, bees, butterflies, various animals to pet, hayfields, pinecones, rocks to roll, sand, snakes, huckleberries and hornets; and any child who has been deprived of these has been deprived . . ."

I love nothing more than letting Mother Nature help me raise my children. I recently took my children to the beach on a chilly day in March. My son wanted to run into the Pacific, and I had to explain that the water is cold in the winter. Meanwhile my daughter was behind me waddling and crawling in the wet sand, putting seaweed into her mouth and reaching for a jellyfish which also must have looked to her like a yummy snack. Last I heard, eating a jellyfish is the only thing worse than being stung by one.

As I turned to pull the seaweed out of her hand and yank her away from the jellyfish, my son scampered free toward the freezing waves. All of that happened in about ten seconds.

Nature has a way of educating and entertaining and bonding.

A little while later, the three of us climbed back into the car, cold, sandy, and very much at peace.

There is nothing like the waves and the wind or the trails and the mud or whatever way nature meets you. It's a simple shift of our attention toward love and light.

We are all innately fluent in that language. Some of us go years without practicing, while others speak that language poetically.

At 94 years old, Ina can no longer stand up straight. Her words, which may or may not make sense, are a faint whisper. She is not going to reach out and grab you with a beautiful Instagram post or podcast interview.

Is she an old lady taking up valuable real estate?

Or is she a sage speaking a timeless language?

It's all a matter of judgment.

"My grandpa, Donald True, lived to be 86. He taught me that motion doesn't equal progress. He was a farmer who understood the value of time. I never saw him run, or seem stressed, or anxious. Instead my grandpa smiled often, laughed easily, and relied upon his faith when the rains didn't come, or came too often. He had a ready smile, two attentive ears to hear what the words could not but the heart longed to say. My grandpa taught me to live in the moment with a hope for the future."

—Debbie, Palmer, Alaska

5

RAGE AGAINST THE LIGHT

Then death comes at dawn, and you wake up laughing at what you thought was your grief.

—*Rumi*

It's rare that 215,000,000 Americans bear witness to the same event.

That's how many Americans looked up at the sky on August 21, 2017, and witnessed the total eclipse of the sun.

I led a retreat with twenty-five people to witness the eclipse on a vineyard in the Willamette Valley, near Salem, Oregon. It was a normal, sunny summer morning until 9:05 a.m. PST when you looked through your eclipse glasses and saw the first tiny sliver of the moon covering the sun.

Over the coming minutes, the skies shifted from a dusk-like yellow and orange to a surreal red and purple.

As the sun faded behind the moon, the temperature dropped from the high 70s down into the 60s. Clouds appeared out of thin air. The confused hawks circled in the sky above, unsure why their ever-dependable sun was disappearing in the middle of the day.

I walked up a hill with a few people, including a few of my oldest friends, to get the best possible view.

The shadow of totality began on the western horizon and moved east at 2,400 miles per hour. The whole experience was otherworldly.

With the winds blowing, the animals howling, the colors shifting, I stood next to one of my very best friends. He said, "This is primal. Dig your feet into the earth. This won't be real unless you ground it!"

We took off our shoes and began digging our feet into the earth as quickly as possible.

A total eclipse is emotionally charged for almost everyone. But my friend's mother had just been removed from life support a few days prior. He was in the throes of grief, mixed with the exultation of this natural phenomenon.

At 10:17 a.m., the sun was seconds from disappearing entirely behind the moon. My friend, through his tears, said, "I think this is what my mom saw when she was dying. Her light was fading . . . just like this."

I had witnessed a total eclipse once before in 1991, and I knew what was coming. I put my hand on my friend's shoulder and told him, "Just wait. Something amazing is about to happen."

At 10:18 a.m., the last little sliver of sunlight disappeared. There was a brief moment of darkness, and then . . . the rarest, most precious ring of light, the corona, suddenly surrounded the moon. The corona is only visible to the human eye during a total eclipse.

I dropped to my knees and felt the texture of the cool, soft earth as this surreal Martian orange sky illuminated the horizon in every direction.

NASA expert Fred Espenak has a rating scheme for natural wonders. He said, "On a scale of 1 to 10, total eclipses are a million." Combine the sheer wonder with my friend's outpouring of emotion, and I was completely unhinged.

The Buddha said, "Three things cannot long be hidden. The sun, the moon, and the truth."

All that comes together during a total eclipse. It's the feeling of being totally at peace.

And then it was over.

Less than two minutes after totality, the sun reappeared, the temperature rose, and it was back to normal. All 25 people in our group, not to mention many of the 215,000,000 Americans who witnessed the total eclipse of the sun, will forever remember.

But for my friend who just lost his mother, it was something greater, a little hint that when things go black, and the light is gone, there might be something unimaginably spectacular yet to come.

Death is the greatest mystery of life. What comes next?

I often ask elders if they are scared of death.

When you are talking to someone in their 90s or 100s, death could come with their very next breath. And yet, not one time did an elder tell me they feared death. And many times, the elders welcomed it with a feisty, festive spirit.

You've probably read the famous poem by Dylan Thomas.

Do not go gentle into that good night,. . .

Rage, rage against the dying of the light.

◆ ◆ ◆ ◆

I met Dr. Bob Stecker, 89, at our Drinks with Your Elders event in Houston. This man epitomizes the meaning of that Dylan Thomas poem: don't die easily. Don't give up too soon.

Dr. Bob's voice may sound tired and hoarse, and he tends to run out of breath. He has a leaky valve in his heart and his lungs are compromised. At first encounter, I thought he was not long for the earth.

But as I have learned, one's physical condition does not necessarily speak to the condition of their will and spirit. As Dr. Bob told me, "My best is yet to come!"

He started his career as a family and marriage therapist and went on to get another degree in Transitional Transformation.

To this day, at 89, he coaches people on death and the changes that happen throughout life: divorce, career change, loss of a spouse, letting go of the past and embracing the present.

When his wife died of breast cancer in 1980, Dr. Bob went to a therapist and said, "I am responsible for my wife's death. I feel terribly guilty that I didn't do more for her."

The therapist sat across from him for a long time and just remained silent. Finally, he said to Dr. Bob, sarcastically, "This is the first time I have counseled a murderer."

It was a strange but effective lesson: "Lose your guilt. It doesn't serve anyone."

But Dr. Bob firmly believes that struggle, if not guilt, is integral to embracing change. He shared the example of a caterpillar.

"A caterpillar needs to eat three or four times its weight in food. It builds a cocoon and dissolves. Out of that ooze comes a butterfly. It has everything it needs to make the transition from a caterpillar. It strengthens its wings by struggling to get out of the cocoon.

"My job is not to tell people how to make a transition, but to help them find what they have within them to make the transition. They have the answers within them. They are not aware they have them."

His advice with divorce is, "Don't get into a committed relationship for a year after. It takes that long to breathe. In the Jewish faith, you don't set a tombstone for a year after someone's death because it takes a year of grieving. If you don't grieve, it catches up with you. You either feel pain now or pain later. If you choose pain later, there's an interest rate."

He also knows a thing or two about staying married. In Dr. Bob's previous career, he was a marriage therapist. He said, "Wouldn't it be wonderful if a couple came to therapy and could look at it as an education process and get a master's degree in their relationship?"

That advice reframed my perspective on my own marriage. In some ways, my wife and I are complete opposites. When we resist and complain about the struggle and our differences, it's very difficult.

Dr. Bob said, "The butterfly has to struggle to get out of the cocoon. It's in the struggle we grow. After struggle, there is a turning point. That's the model of marriage. Honor the struggle, instead of trying to get rid of it."

Someone in the audience at the Drinks with Your Elders event asked Dr. Bob, "But does all this change get easier as you get older?"

He said, "No! Change is everything. It doesn't get easier. You get stronger and more efficient."

Now, this might not answer any questions about death. But studying the process of change as it occurs throughout life prepares us for the biggest transition of all. While 215,000,000 Americans saw the eclipse, all 7 billion people on the planet will one day experience their death. Is it a glorious spectacle like the eclipse or something entirely different?

Dr. Bob believes part of death is how you approach it. We can deny and avoid our mortality, which he says makes us elderly. Or we can accept our mortality and, let go of our tug-of-war with life, and that makes you an elder.

Your process begins now. With every moment of change, every transition that comes your way:

You see the ending, or a new beginning.

You fear change, or you welcome it.

You become elderly, or you become an elder.

"My Baba Nesse Godin, who is 90 years old, is the person who inspires me the most. She is still living. A survivor of the Holocaust, she taught me to speak up, make sure people around me feel and are treated equally, and not to stay silent."
—Miri, Middleton, Wisconsin

6

WHEN I ARRIVED IN AUSCHWITZ

Without memory, there is no culture. Without memory, there would be no civilization, no society, no future.
—Elie Wiesel, Holocaust survivor and Nobel Laureate

Of all the conversation with elders, my most shocking occurred on a flight to Chicago. I sat next to an elder couple, Helga, 84, and Hans, 82. Helga did all the talking, and she told me how they immigrated from Germany to the United States in the 1950s.

I asked Helga if she remembered the Nazis. She said, ashamedly, "I was part of the Hitler Youth."

The Hitler Youth?

I had met Holocaust survivors and heard stories of survival, but I had never met someone in the Hitler Youth, the daughter of Nazis. I started poking and prodding, and Helga kept talking.

She recalled how, during the war, her Jewish neighbors just started disappearing. She was told they were being "resettled."

"Anything to drink?" the flight attendant asked, which brought me back to reality, at least for a moment. I was transfixed by this conversation. The Hitler Youth?

In the years after the war, Helga said she felt such terrible shame when telling people she was German.

There are so many perspectives on how World War II impacted the Silent Generation, which is made up of people born between 1920-1942.

An elder I met in Chicago, Ruth, 93, recalled the day Pearl Harbor was attacked. Her senior prom was canceled because her entire senior class was about to be shipped off to war.

Another lady in Salt Lake City said, "all the beautiful boys" from her freshman class in college went to fight in the war, and only half of them came back.

A veteran in Dallas told me he was serving in Hawaii the morning of December 7, 1941. He remembered the thick black smoke rising over the USS Arizona.

Helga recalled the memory of her hometown Stuttgart, in the aftermath of the war, on fire, burning to nothing. She said, "It's still fresh in my mind."

And then there was Alice, a Holocaust survivor, who shared the raw pain and horror of Auschwitz.

◆ ◆ ◆ ◆

An old college friend sent me a message:

"Alice is 89 years old, and is a Holocaust survivor. She lives in LA now and has kids and a grandson. She still talks about it and has returned to Germany and Budapest a few times since."

This friend picked me up on a cool, rainy day in October 2016. We drove down a canyon into Alice's lovely neighborhood. Considering that a third of American Holocaust survivors are living in poverty, it seemed that Alice was fortunate. But I was about to learn that word does not make sense to her.

Alice answered the door and welcomed us. Her Hungarian accent is still very prominent. Before we sat down, I noticed a mural covering an entire wall of her kitchen. This mural told the story of Alice's life. It started on the far left with the year 1927 and happy images before the war. Scanning to the right, the images portrayed her life growing up in Hungary in 1939, and haunting images of the loved ones she lost in the Holocaust in 1941. Further to the right were post-war images of her husband and children in 1956 and subsequent trips to Israel in 1991. The mural told the story all the way through 2012.

Alice sat down across from us and without pleasantries or small talk, she started telling her story.

"My father taught me that the Jewish people are God's favorite people. When I arrived in Auschwitz I thought, *favorite for what? favorite for murder?*"

Alice grew up in Hungary until she was 16.

"My father was a tailor. He was killed two years before Auschwitz. My grandparents were growing fruit and supplied the whole country with apples. My father was helping his parents to deliver a wagon full of apples. These horrendous Hungarian hoodlums, young people who were totally anti-Semitic, ordered my father off the road. All the apples fell all over the street. They brought him into the building in a railroad station and beat him up."

Alice's mother took her severely injured father to the best doctors to have him examined.

"They went to a doctor in another country but I found out my mother took him home in a box."

She remembers, "Somebody came in a horse and carriage and took us to my father's funeral. It wouldn't have mattered if he lived. He would have gone to Auschwitz and died with everyone else. I have nobody."

Alice finished each of these sentences with a moment of silence. It felt like she had told this story many times. She was hardened to the raw emotions. There were no tears. But there was a kind of deep, old, terrible pain that she somehow learned to live with.

Alice explained that Hungary was a 98% Catholic country. "All Sunday they go to church. Monday they were ready to kill a Jew anytime. I remember the people in their homes applauding as the SS marched us through the streets to the railroad station.

"I was 16. I had no idea where I was. Why did I come? After three days of traveling in a horrible bus, we arrived [at Auschwitz]. There was no food, no bathroom. I was with my mother, two brothers, two sisters. My mother carried my three-and-a-half-year-old beautiful little sister. Then I was carrying her because my mother was busy with the boys. When the door opened, the Sonderkommandos [work units made up of prisoners] said, 'Give the baby to your mother.'"

Alice's life was saved by this Sonderkommando, but the rest of her family was sent to the gas chamber.

"The SS put me to work, picking up stone from one place and putting it to the other place. Useless things.

"One day I found three cousins. Their father and my father were twins. We looked after each other. It was just horrendous. Somehow we survived."

After the war, Alice met her husband, who had survived the war, living on the streets of Budapest. He had managed to evade the Nazis. Alice and her husband emigrated to the United States, moved to Los Angeles, and had two children.

"When I was married, I felt safe and happy. I had hardly any money for groceries. My husband made sixty or sixty-five dollars a week. But I was happy. I didn't have my parents anymore, but I had a wonderful family.

"My husband was really special. When I was pregnant, my husband didn't want me to take my shower alone because he wanted to make sure I didn't fall down. He would be with me in the shower and wash me and kiss me and wash me and kiss me. I always loved fruit. So he would go to the market and buy me all kinds of fruit. I was in bed for weeks with morning sickness, and he would buy me the fruit. I would throw it up from morning sickness. But the very next day he'd go back and buy me the fruit I felt like having. That's how loving and good of a person my husband was.

"Goodness gracious he was such a wonderful father and husband."

Her husband died suddenly at the age of 55.

"I was double angry at God. Why would God take him away? You took away my whole family and now you took away my husband?

"Then I got an idea that I'm gonna travel and visit the places in the world that are beautiful because I saw too many ugly things in this world. I went to 45 countries, some of which I've been back two or three or four times.

"Many years later I went back to Hungary to show my children where I came from. I didn't remember the house in my hometown. When I lived there, the front area was gardens. Now it's planted full of houses. An elderly man was walking in the street. I said to my daughter, 'Let's ask this man. Maybe he remembers my father.'

"In Hungarian, I politely told him I am the daughter of a man who used to live here but I don't remember which house. I want to show my children.

He said, 'Are you looking for the Jewish house?'

I said, 'Yes.'

"He pointed to the house. Then he looked me in the face, 'Isn't that wonderful how we got rid of the Jews?'

"My daughter was so mad. I said to my angry daughter, 'Sweetheart, just see where it's coming from.'"

Alice continues to have nightmares about walking in the street looking for her family.

"I forget about yesterday, and just an hour ago, and what I did or didn't do, or what I should do. But I can't forget what happened those years."

You hear these Holocaust stories in books and on TV. But it was entirely different to sit in the room with an 89-year-old as she described handing her three-and-a-half-year-old sister to her mother and then watching them march to their death. As I write this, my son is that same age. How can human beings become such monsters?

And to think Alice came from a well-to-do family in a beautiful European capital. The next thing she knew, they were being paraded through the streets of her hometown, with their neighbors applauding as they were being rounded up for death?

Here we were, in this beautiful enclave of a neighborhood in Southern California, and here was this 89-year-old woman living among us, still suffering the pain of losing all ten of her family members in the Holocaust, including both sets of grandparents, her parents, and four siblings.

I went back and visited Alice a few weeks later. I wanted to do something, offer her something. She has two children and one grandchild, but I still wanted to let her know I cared. Not that I expected to change her outlook, but maybe it would help for her to know that someone she is not related to sees her and hears her.

She asked if I could take her to temple one Saturday afternoon. I enthusiastically jumped at the opportunity and took her for several hours to her local Chabad.

But I still hadn't seen her smile. I wondered if there was something more I could do to bring her a little joy?

I brought my then-two-year-old son to meet Alice. He waddled into her home, instantly gravitated toward her wireless phone, and started pushing the buttons. Anything with buttons. Alice did not have any young grandchildren in her life, so the energy of a toddler uplifted her. It was the first time I saw her smile.

What does a two-year-old know except joy and tears and sleep and love and ice cream?

Speaking of which, my son and I came back with a piece of ice cream cake to celebrate Alice's 90th birthday. I'd like to think that a two-year-old's purity gave Alice a glimmer of hope for humanity.

I took a picture of my son with Alice. One day, when he is old enough, I'll tell him about that picture. I'll tell him Alice's story.

I also took a picture of Helga who spoke of the Hitler Youth. I'll show my son that picture and tell him about Helga's story. She was only a child during the war, and was not guilty of the crimes committed by her countrymen.

We all start so young and so innocent. May we capture that energy, that spirit of the very young, and spread it to the very old, to the prejudiced and imprisoned, to the world leaders, to the brokenhearted, to those who have lost faith and lost trust.

Not to say this will relieve Alice of her pain. But at the very least, I want her to know, this is my commitment: to ensure that her lessons and story will live on in the hearts of the younger generations. That our children will be shaped by her pain, humbled by her losses, strengthened by her resilience.

"My grandmother raised two very young kids in Germany during the Second World War. She was part of the German underground, saving American and Allied soldiers' lives. She had a blouse made from the parachute of an American solider who was dropped behind enemy lines. There are so many stories about the things she had to do to protect her family. She was thrown in jail and tortured for refusing to give the Nazi salute. Fortunately, the Americans liberated her town after she was put in jail. She probably would not have survived otherwise. She taught me: Be principled and strong as hell!"

—Rob, New York City

7

BE HAPPY (right this second)

If you must look back, do so forgivingly. If you must look forward, do so prayerfully. However, the wisest thing you can do is be present in the present . . . gratefully.

—*Maya Angelou*

I asked one of my close friends about his biggest fear. He answered, "That I will not fulfill my potential."

God forbid you leave something on the table and think back on what you coulda, woulda, shoulda. Every business coach, sports coach, self-help guru, and motivational speaker pushes us in the direction of our potential.

What if they have it all wrong? What if life is not about potential?

Marianne Williamson writes that there is a huge difference between potential and capacity:

". . . Potential can be a dangerous concept . . . We're constantly measuring ourselves against what we think we could be, rather than what we are.

"Capacity is expressed in the present, it is immediate. The key to it lies not in what we have inside of us, but rather in what we are willing to own that we have inside of us."

That's the story of Jack, 104 years old!

Jack's daughter Lotus reached out to me with this introduction: "If you'd like to meet or speak with my father, I know he'd be happy to do so . . . his mind is good and his attitude is still fabulous."

It's rare enough to meet a centenarian, someone who is 100 or older. Centenarians comprise just 0.02 percent of the US population, or 55,000 people. It's rarer to meet a male centenarian. Males make up only about 20% of that 55,000. A male centenarian is somewhat of a genetic freak. As Dr. Thomas Perls of the Boston Medical Center said, "People who live into their 90s are totally different from people who live to be 100 or 105."

In such rare encounters with a male centenarian, let alone one who is four years past the 100 mark, I'm looking for their secret sauce.

With Jack, you don't look. He'll tell you:

"Life is to be enjoyed! The reason for my longevity is a positive attitude. It's the most important thing one can have. Get rid of negativity."

I asked him how to do that.

"It's not hard. You have to think in a positive light. I had a hard life. I worked two jobs most of my life. But I enjoyed it because I was positive."

Jack was born on August 13, 1913. One of his first memories was the night when the armistice was signed to end World War I. He was six years old, living in Harlem on 112th

Street off 8th Avenue, two blocks north of Central Park and two blocks east of Morningside Park. "People were throwing furniture off the roof and burning it in the middle of the street [to celebrate]."

He grew up working for his parents in the grocery business. Then he ran his own grocery store before getting a job as a salesman by day and a clerk at a harness racing track by night. For thirty-two years, he worked two jobs, rising early and not getting home until 1:00 a.m.

He remembers in vivid detail his wedding day in 1937 in the Bronx.

"I can picture the entire thing, the dinner we had, all the people who were there. My brother-in-law wanted to hand out cigars but I wouldn't let him because I knew he'd pocket them."

Jack and his wife had two children, one grandchild, one great-grandchild, and twin great-grandchildren on the way. His wife passed away in 1990 at 75 years old. "We had a fantastic marriage."

I asked if losing his wife was a setback. "I lived the same life, just without her. Never married again."

He did continue dating. He has outlived three or four women in the almost thirty years since he lost his wife. In fact, Jack said he has outlived almost everyone he has known.

"You miss them at the beginning and then they fade to the background and you have a daily life that takes its place."

Like many of the elders who reach very old age and keep on keepin' on, Jack is able to shift his attention toward something useful.

"Forget the past unless you can use it. Don't think of the past 'I coulda, shoulda, woulda, oughta.' The only way you can use it is remembering good things that happened or that you made a mistake you can learn from."

Along with the attitude comes his regimen.

Jack goes to the gym for over an hour, two to four times each week. He only takes one medication. He has the blood pressure of a 20-year-old. He has no heart condition. He lives alone. And he still drives!

"Evidently I'm doing something right."

I asked how old he feels.

"I don't give age a thought at all. I don't really understand what 104 is. I live from day to day and try to enjoy every day the best I can."

I said, "Wow!"

He replied, "No wow! Open your eyes and look for things to be good. Keep your mind on being positive. Get away from negativity and everything is automatically good. Minimize the bad side. We have our bad times. We have to live through them. But don't make it worse than it is."

Three weeks after my conversation with Jack, I enjoyed a pre-dawn taxi ride from my hotel on the big island of Hawaii to the airport in Kona.

I sipped on a delicious cup of Kona coffee. A warm tropical wind blew through the open windows. Hawaii has a sweet, floral scent that overcomes you. I felt the most wonderful sense of contentment, presence.

I kept saying to myself, "I gotta keep this feeling with me when I get home. It feels so good. If I could feel this way more often, I would have it made."

And then I started asking, praying, "God, how do I keep this feeling with me?"

I got on the plane for my connecting flight from Kona to Honolulu. A lady sat down next to me. She was accompanied by a very big service dog, about the size of a Golden Retriever. I'm not particularly a dog person.

As I stood up to let the lady and her dog shuffle into their seat by the window, the dog jumped onto my seat and lay down. The lady had to nudge her dog off my seat and into the tiny area by her feet.

This lady was so nice and so concerned that I would be annoyed with her dog. The flight attendant came over to oversee this arrangement. Passengers all around us were watching, trying to figure out if I was going to object.

But this dog was special. It put its head on my lap and kissed my hand and kept trying to jump up onto me.

I mean . . . I had no leg room at all. No room to move. And I am *not* a dog person.

But this was the answer to my question, "How do I keep this feeling?"

In that moment, I heard one voice saying, "You should complain. This is ridiculous. It's not fair."

That was the voice of "potential" telling me there is something better for me to strive for in this moment. There's always something better, a way to improve, grow, increase.

But I also heard a voice saying, "All this dog knows is love and it's directing it toward me with drool and dog hair and a tongue that doesn't stop licking."

That was the voice of "capacity" telling me there is love in this moment, and maybe I could get more from this furry creature than I could from two inches of legroom and a dirty table on which to put my coffee.

Which voice was I going to listen to in that moment?

You might have this debate going on in your mind. There's something you are striving for. A promotion. A better physique. A more attentive partner. That's the voice of potential telling you there is always something better.

There's something right in front of your right now to enjoy and embrace. Your health and mobility. Your job that keeps the jangle flowing. The delicious glass of red wine. That's the voice of capacity saying, "Dude! Right here. Right now."

In that moment, on that plane, with that dog slobbering all over me, I gave a nod to Jack, and a high five to capacity.

I traded legroom for love; and one lukewarm cup of airline coffee for 100 licks from that all-time most lovable dog.

Looking forward, it might not sound like much. Looking back, it's the best trade I ever made.

"My grandma Eleanor is still alive at 95 years old. She has taught me that the human mind doesn't always keep up with the body. I am writing things down and taking pictures so if I get to be that age, I will be able to remember and share my past."
—Eric, Los Angeles, California

8

ACCESS YOUR
HIDDEN POWER

*Throw your dreams into space like a kite, and you do not know
what it will bring back: a new life, a new friend, a new love,
a new country.*

—*Anaïs Nin*

You know those books that change your life and give you
a supercharge?

The Power of Intention by the late Wayne Dyer revealed a
kind of human superpower. I remember reading this book and
thinking, *Oh this is awesome and so true and why didn't I know
about this?!* Every page was thunder and lighting and revelation!

Wayne Dyer writes, "Intention is not something you do,
but rather a force that exists in the universe as an invisible
field of energy."

And if you choose to access this field of energy, you tap
into what Indian sage Patanjali described as "dormant forces,
faculties, and talents" and you become "a greater person by far
than you ever dreamed yourself to be."

How do you access this field of energy? Ask yourself, before you do something, "What do I intend to happen?"

Oprah credits her understanding of intention with changing her whole life. She said, "Before there is a cause or effect, there is an intention, a true reason for wanting to do things. If you look at what the intention is in every circumstance in your life, the energy of your intention is what actually creates the effect. I use this for everything in my life."

When you have a heartfelt intention behind your actions, you tap into this field of energy. You set into motion a highly charged series of events, aligned with love and truth, health and prosperity.

Before setting out to write this book, I got very clear on my intention. I intend that these elders' stories be heard by the younger generations. I intend that these stories add value and meaning to your life. I intend that someone reading this, maybe you, will be inspired to deepen or discover relationships with the elders in your world.

Along the way, I learned that when you consciously access the power of intention, doors will open. Teachers will appear.

◆　◆　◆　◆

My stepfather invited me to join him and a 92-year-old World War II veteran, Seymour, at a ceremony in downtown Los Angeles honoring surviving recipients of the Medal of Honor. There are only seventy-five Americans alive today who have received this honor for acts of valor.

On the car ride, Seymour shared his story of serving on a submarine in the South Pacific during World War II.

Seymour recalled, "We were between the Philippines and Okinawa, headed back to Midway on a war patrol. We got caught. The waves were forty or fifty feet high. We tried to get down below the surface but the water was so vicious it threw us back up on the surface. It got so nasty. We finally got down. The whole fleet was caught in that. It was a horrible, horrible mess. You can't get out of it. You are trapped."

He was referring to Typhoon Cobra, whose 140 mph winds sunk three US destroyers and claimed the lives of 790 US servicemen.

He shared a look into life on an enclosed metal tube hundreds of feet below the ocean with other eighteen-, nineteen-, and twenty-year-old Americans hoping to survive a war that claimed 80 million people across the earth. It was a brutal time to be alive.

If I did nothing more that night than have that conversation with Seymour and my stepfather for the hour-long drive, that would have made for an intriguing and enlightening hour of American history. But the night was just beginning.

As we arrived at the Jonathan Club in downtown Los Angeles, we mingled with some of the Medal of Honor recipients including Thomas Norris and Michael Thornton.

These are not your everyday heroes, and it is something special to be in a room with these men. For instance, take the story of Norris and Thornton.

In October 1972, Norris and Thornton were caught behind enemy lines in North Vietnam.

For four hours, they held off an enemy force estimated at about 200-300 strong. Norris called in naval firepower on the enemy's positions, helping to keep his fellow men alive.

But the North Vietnamese regrouped and surrounded the troops.

Norris was shot in the head and severely wounded. Thornton, upon hearing the news, ran through heavy fire to recover the body of his fallen comrade. He killed several North Vietnamese as they surmounted the dunes around his position and then carried the unconscious Norris into the water.

Thornton also carried one of the South Vietnamese soldiers who had been wounded and was unable to swim into the ocean. Thornton swam and supported the two injured men for more than two hours before they were picked up by the same junk which had dropped them off the night before.

Norris lost an eye and part of his skull. He spent three years recovering from his injuries in the hospital, and over a six-year period underwent many major surgeries.

Thornton was recognized with the Medal of Honor for his actions by President Richard Nixon during a ceremony at the White House on October 15, 1973. He snuck Norris out of the hospital in the middle of the night to attend his Medal of Honor ceremony.

Norris was later awarded the Medal of Honor by President Gerald R. Ford in a White House ceremony on March 6, 1976.

I was excited to spend an evening with Seymour and my stepfather, and meet these incredible Medal of Honor recipients. Maybe get a picture, ask a few questions. If nothing more, their stories captivated and thrilled, and I felt honored to be in the same room.

As the dinner began, my mom called. She was babysitting my then-two-year-old son back in Encino. It turns out she could not find his blankie, and he refused to go to sleep without it.

I told her on the phone, "Mom, he'll be fine, I'm at a Medal of Honor dinner. I'm not coming home because he can't find his blankie. C'mon mom. He's two. You can do this."

It may not be comparable to that of Thomas Norris and Michael Thornton, but the will of a two-year-old who cannot find his blankie is a force of nature!

Lo and behold, a few minutes later, I sat, disgruntled, in the back of an Uber on the way to my mom's house to pick up my son and take him home to get his backup blankie.

I looked at the Uber driver's phone mounted atop his console. It showed one hour of gridlock traffic to get to my mom's house.

It didn't take the Uber driver more than a few minutes before he began to tell me a story about the old days, when he used to drive a taxi. He proceeded to tell me that one of his passengers held him at gunpoint. Mind you, I come from the wellness world so I usually talk about mantras and athleisure trends rather than guns and war and battles. But it seemed that guns were the theme of this particular evening.

The Uber driver continued, "My passenger had a gun to my head. He told me to get out of the car and climb in the trunk.

"I pleaded with him. 'You took my money. You took my stuff. You can take my car. Please just don't take my life. Let me go home to my family.'

"The guy demanded that I climb into the trunk. He pointed his gun at me. I made my peace with God. I said 'God, if you say it's my time, please take me. I'm ready.'

"I was waiting to hear the gunshots and I was sure my life was over.

"But the guy closed the trunk, trapped me in there, and kept driving. Thirty or so minutes later, he pulled the taxi over. He let me go.

"I got to live and I knew I had to do something different, more meaningful with my life!"

This Uber driver shared with me how this lifechanging event turned him into an inspirational speaker. He now preaches to Latin-American families about the power of *waking up* and embracing a goal-driven life.

This Uber driver now shares the message with as many people as possible. He is a healer to his community. The more people he talks to, the more suicides he prevents, the more addicts he turns toward rehab, the more downtrodden passengers he uplifts with his story.

His name was Ascension. Of course.

As Ascension pulled up to my mom's house, I was no longer frustrated about leaving Seymour and the Medal of Honor dinner. It was clear I had a more important place to be—hearing from a man who was awakened to his purpose.

This made me think. If I was held at gunpoint, certain I was going to die, and I was allowed to live, how would that change me? How would that change you?

What has to happen to awaken me, to awaken you, to the meaning of life?

You know Martin Luther King Jr.'s quote, "I can never be what I ought to be until you are what you ought to be, and you can never be what you ought to be until I am what I ought to be . . ."

Everyone is depending on you and me to wake up, to live up, to what matters most.

The moment we see our life as an honor instead of a grind, the page turns and an opening appears. Or so I am learning.

A conversation with an elder has the potential to open up, and reveal so much more. I would never have received this message from Ascension if not for the intention to spend an evening with 92-year-old Seymour and learn about his story. That intention set in motion a chain of events which I could not have seen coming.

Sometimes we hold so tightly to the endgame that we become blind to everything and everyone happening along the way.

When is the last time you checked in with the question, "What do I intend to happen here?"

Is your career intention strictly to earn money? Or do you intend to help, educate, inspire, improve?

Is your love intention to be attractive and desired? Or do you intend to connect, nurture, elevate?

Is your charitable intention to give as much as possible and be recognized? Or do you intend to link your talent and purpose with those who might benefit most?

When our intention is clear, circumstances change, doors open, teachers appear.

Life stops happening to you and starts happening for you.

"Grandmama—aka Marguerite. She taught me to enjoy the simple pleasures—food from the garden, a new blouse, a good shade of lipstick, a fresh-made lemonade, appreciation for pretty colors like aqua and pink (not "pank") . . . and yes, flowers, flowers, flowers. And hummingbirds. She just died in February and would have been 99. I *love* her. And she had a girl-like giggle even as an old lady. And she was really good at Wheel of Fortune."

—Katie, Birmingham, Alabama

9

CHERISH YOUR MARRIAGE
(before it's too late)

*Suddenly, I'm not half the man I used to be. There's a shadow
hanging over me, oh yesterday came suddenly.*

—*Paul McCartney*

Do you take your partner for granted? Maybe just a little bit?

When the anniversaries start to stack into sets of ten and you get to your second, third, fourth decade . . . that's a long time to be with one person. A *long* time.

I'm only on year seven of my marriage and this I know for sure: my wife and I drive each other certifiably, absolutely, completely insane.

It's the little things, like hearing each other chew too loudly, or when she wants to watch *The Food Network* and I want to watch the College Baseball World Series, or being away from home for several days and she is running wake up and bedtime with a one- and three-year-old. And those are the times when, if there was an eject button, maybe one of us might just brush up against it. Don't tell me you too haven't thought about that.

Nonetheless . . .

I will proudly tell you, my wife is a beautiful, dedicated mom who works her ass off in her career. I am sometimes numb to the delicious pancakes she makes on Saturday mornings and her fetish for clean clothes with no wrinkles, and her undying commitment to raising well-rested, disciplined, well-fed children, and working a full-time job.

But those petty arguments we have with each other take their toll. Our opposing personalities test our patience. And after thirteen years together since our first date, sometimes you run out of things to talk about.

I wish I could be more awake and appreciative of those little (and big) moments we share with our children and each other. There is nothing more sacred. Those moments are everything we live and work for.

How do I wake up from the slow erosion of "same ol' same ol'"? How do I wake up to the blessing of my marriage?

My friend and author Jaimal Yogis tells a story in his book *All Our Waves Are Water* about visiting the Wailing Wall in Israel. He sees all the devout worshippers, and wedges himself into the front row, next to the wall. In the cracks between the gigantic limestone bricks, people stuff pieces of paper, prayers.

Jaimal takes out his reporter's notebook and scribbles down a prayer, "Dear God, Please, I beg you, wake me up!"

He rolls up the paper and slips it into one of the stone cracks. That was that. He turns around to leave but a group of bearded rabbis stands shoulder to shoulder and sways behind him. Jaimal has nowhere to go. He feels awkward. So he places his hand on the limestone and relies on the one Hebrew line he knows, "Baruch atah adonai eloheinu melech haolam—"Blessed are you, the Lord our God, King of the Universe." He gets caught in the fervor and energy and begins to recite it with more and more vigor, louder and louder.

Jaimal writes, "I began to cry, nearly delirious in the power . . . that collapsed in from all sides. The only appropriate response to this power was to wail . . . I could not run. . . . The wall of rabbis barred me in . . . Even though the tears were ecstatic, I tried to resist . . . But when the bawling became uncontrollable . . . the sort that feels like you're finally crying for the pain of the cosmos . . . my intellect gave up."

That's what I'm talkin' about by "waking up." I want to feel that kind of delirious, ecstatic, emotional breakthrough. I want my intellect to give up and my heart to explode.

"Dear God, please, I beg you, wake me up!"

❖　❖　❖　❖

The answer to this prayer came through a conversation with Ron, 81 years old, who presented marriage to me through a completely different lens of perception.

Ron wrote a book, *Time to Say Goodbye*, about the last sixty-one hours he spent with his late wife Joan. He sat in the hospital and held her hand as she lay dying. It all came rushing back in a last crescendo of grief, celebration, joy, and pain.

Over the previous years, Joan had struggled with dementia. She showed the first signs of Alzheimer's in 2006 and passed away due to complications in 2014.

Ron described to me the journey from beginning to end. At first, Joan had a little slip in memory, like putting a pill on the table to take before bedtime and a few moments later, putting another on the table. Then there was an outburst of denial, "I don't have Alzheimer's. I don't have Alzheimer's."

She would greet everyone as though they were a special friend, even people she was meeting for the first time.

After swimming, she dressed quickly, not drying herself properly.

Then came repetitive questions, forgetting how to cook, and when cooking, making a mess in the kitchen only to ask, "Who made this mess? Are you going to clean it up?"

She began to have issues with personal hygiene. As her dementia progressed, she went from a daily shower to twice-weekly, then once each week. Ron had to practically wrestle her to get her undressed, and walk her into the shower. She would turn the shower head away and onto Ron. He'd pretend to be having fun, but this was his wife of fifty-eight years, not a two-year-old. After showering, he'd dress her in night clothes and help her to sleep. It was a relief just to get through a single day.

Eventually, he checked her into a care center at which point her health declined sharply. Countless visits to the emergency room removed the last sparkle from her eyes. She spent most of the day and night in bed. She was fading and Ron was heartbroken.

As Joan took her final breaths, Ron sat next to her, her hand in his, and he shared out loud their memories.

Swimming in the waves in Waikiki.

Golfing in the tropical rain.

Frequenting the Chart House and listening to real Hawaiian music while drinking Budweiser.

Sitting outside their vacation trailer in Banff with a 360-degree panoramic view of the majestic mountains, comfortable in their loungers, sipping on a bottle of fine burgundy.

"We were there to appreciate the natural beauty around us. Some would call it peaceful meditation. There was never much conversation as this was a place of tranquility. Sitting with our backs to the setting sun, we'd marvel at the changing hues."

Meeting for the first time in Blackpool, England, in 1954. Ron remembered dancing with Joan to the song "Hold My Hand" by Don Cornell. They were singing or "belting out" the words and were asked to keep it down. They had so much fun that the next night they went on their first date to see a movie, "On the Waterfront" with Marlon Brando.

In her final hours, Ron kept kissing her on her cheeks, forehead, lips. She was always looking at him. He wondered what was going on behind her eyes.

He sang to her, "Yesterday, all my troubles seemed so far away, now it looks as though they're here to stay, oh I believe in yesterday."

She died on Easter Sunday 2014.

I was so sad listening to Ron's story. I could relate to his memories, watching sunsets, remembering my first date with my wife in 2005. We went to Maha Yoga and Nagao for sushi before watching an episode of *Curb Your Enthusiasm*. That's when we had our first kiss. We still argue all the time about who initiated that first kiss.

How do we get back to that early stage of desire?

Allow yourself to see your own relationship through Ron's lens.

Imagine yourself at some point in the distant future, holding your partner's hand as they lie dying. Imagine your grief. Imagine thinking back on the deep love and appreciation for this person with whom you journeyed through the years and decades, greeting your newborn, changing diapers, filling lunchboxes, helping with homework, driving to practices and rehearsals, traveling the world, helping each other through loss and change and despair, dancing at concerts, watching sunsets, making love.

All of it coming back to you in this final moment as you say goodbye. What would you express to your partner in that final moment? How would you touch them? Would you want to be alone or surrounded by family?

Every so often, change your lens of perception. See through the eyes of an elder looking back, saying goodbye.

And repeat.

"Dear God, please, I beg you, wake me up!"

"I just spent the weekend visiting my 97-year-old mother. She has taught me the power of optimism and gratitude in aging gracefully. She is truly a joy to be around. Even as her body is failing her, she is grateful for things I take for granted, like waking up without pain and a good night's sleep. She is a wonderful example of positivity and grace, which just happens to be her name."

—Pamela, Jackson, Tennessee

10

THE CURE FOR LONELINESS

The most terrible poverty is loneliness and the feeling of being unloved.

—*Mother Teresa*

What does your "loneliness" sound like?

I know a kind of loneliness that whispers in my ear:

"You don't have time to talk to people. Get back to your computer, you lazy-ass!"

"I know it's a beautiful day to have lunch with a friend, but that's what the weekend is for!"

"Downtime with a loved one? Dude, you have bills to pay!"

It pushes me to stick to my computer and focus, focus, focus! It's mean-spirited, very demanding, and toxic.

According to a study by the University of Cambridge, sustained loneliness is twice as dangerous as obesity. And the increased mortality risk of loneliness is equal to that of smoking.

You might be thinking, *I'm not lonely so this doesn't apply to me. This only applies to those people who spend all night surfing the web or watching QVC.*

But can you say the same for your partner or your kids or your best friend?

The Harvard Business Review reports, "Over 40% of adults in America report feeling lonely."

I posted on Facebook: What does loneliness feel like in your life? These were some of the answers:

"Loneliness comes from feeling disconnected to Source, self, and others."

"Loneliness comes from expecting others to make sure I am not lonely."

"Sometimes I feel most lonely with someone who doesn't treat me well."

"Loneliness is when it becomes habit to not do something for someone else."

"Real loneliness for me is when no one hears me or tries to understand what I'm saying."

"I feel lonely for the way I thought things and people should be."

The answers kept on coming, from all across the planet. In fact, loneliness is such an issue, Britain has appointed a Minister for Loneliness. And the former Surgeon General of the United States, Vivek Murthy, said, "During my years caring for patients, the most common pathology I saw was not heart disease or diabetes; it was loneliness."

It starts when we are kids. I remember some of my loneliest moments when I was twelve and thirteen years old. I wasn't part of the "cool crowd." My parents went out to dinner with friends and my little brother was out with friends, and here I was at home, watching *Saturday Night Live*, by myself.

Loneliness receded over time but still rears its head in moments of uncertainty.

It's mostly manageable when you are young. You can work through the argument with your spouse. The holiday weekend when you had no plans will soon be over. The difficult winter will give way to a beautiful spring.

But when you are older, loneliness can be oppressive. It's much harder to shake the blues when you are struggling to move your aching body, or talk after suffering a stroke, or breathe through your emphysema.

Before reading any further, I want to tell you: there is light at the end of this tunnel!

But the secret lies in what many consider the darkest place.

At a Drinks with Your Elders event in New York City, Roberta took us to this darkest place.

Only 71, she has been through ten lifetimes of bad luck. Once upon a time, she had a successful career in editing at Rodale.

"I did very, very well. I kept being promoted. I enjoyed my job tremendously. I had a staff. In the 90s, we were downsized. It was a complete shock.

"If I didn't get another job right away, I'd get a year of severance so I stayed until the end and lived comfortably for a year."

Note: You are about to hear a death-defying, vicious freefall. This is not for the faint of heart.

Roberta continued, "I was freelancing and writing books and doing very well. In 2005, I had a terrible case of pneumonia which turned into asthma and lung disease. Then I got sick with endometrial cancer in 2007. I couldn't afford health insurance. I ended up in the hospital and I went bankrupt. It was thousands and thousands and thousands of dollars.

"I recovered but had another surgery for a hernia. Then in 2010, I was diagnosed with throat cancer. I didn't have money. I went to the cancer clinic. There was a lawyer who helped me get Medicaid. I had eight weeks of radiation on my throat which was the most horrible experience. I could not swallow or talk. They gave me intravenous liquids. While this was happening, I had an asthma attack and was hospitalized and pumped full of steroids.

"When I got out of the hospital I had an amnesia attack and I went to the ER and they realized I had a brain tumor. So after they finished radiation for my throat, then I had surgery on my brain. I'm very pragmatic. I just deal with things as they come. But the brain tumor scared the hell out of me. I could live with the other stuff. But not without a brain.

"As a result of radiation on my throat, I could no longer use my vocal cords. Then I had brain surgery and radiation on my brain.

"Then they found a growth on my throat which had to be removed so I had surgery for that. Then I found out that I had breast cancer and I had surgery and radiation on that. Meanwhile my lung disease became emphysema. More recently I've been diagnosed with spinal stenosis which causes me pain in my neck and back, and peripheral neuropathy which affects my balance. So if I don't hang onto something, I fall down.

"I felt like my body was my enemy. I had to deal with what I had to deal with. One of the problems people with cancer have is they lose friends—I lost all of my friends."

Okay . . . take a second to breathe.

As Roberta paused, I studied the audience at this Drinks with Your Elders. The vibe in the room was dark and heavy, yet deeply engaging, like a Stephen King thriller. Life turned on this lady Roberta and seemed to be attacking her. And yet, here she was, a survivor!

It's a cautionary tale on the precious value of good health. In your older age, life can take a quick turn for the worse. And no matter your ambition or resilience or professional significance, if your health gives out, you can't always outmuscle or outshine your circumstances. You need people to show up for you.

Roberta never married and never had children. She lives alone.

She said, "I feel invisible. Partly because of my age. Partly because of technology. I get in the elevator or the bus and everyone is looking at their phone. Nobody is looking up.

"I feel irrelevant. Young people have very little interest in the past and feel old people are just annoying. I feel like a speed bump. New York City is very fast paced. People walk fast. Now when I'm walking down the street, people are walking around me trying to get past me. I feel like I slow people down. It makes me self-conscious that I'm slow."

One woman at the Drinks with Your Elders event started crying. She couldn't take it anymore. Too many body blows. Her tears broke the emotional silence and burst the bubble. Everyone in the room exhaled and felt closer to Roberta. She needed to unleash. And we needed to hear it.

You might not be able to prevent cancer and certain health struggles that come with aging. But every single one of us can takes steps to heal loneliness.

Roberta said to everyone in the room, "Stop texting and talk to each other."

We all live in our bubbles. We go about our routines. We interact with the same family members and coworkers each and every day. It's so easy to pay no attention to the fact that people like Roberta are all around us, enduring a terrible loneliness. She lives smack in the middle of the biggest city in one of the biggest countries. But Roberta spends most of her time alone, feeling invisible.

Now you might be thinking, *I'm doing the best I can to work and support a family. How am I supposed to have time for the Robertas of the world?*

Or you might be thinking, *I've got enough problems in my life. If I'm going to hang out with an elder, at least let it be a positive one.*

The sages teach, "You reap what you sow."

Call it karma, call it what you will.

I strongly believe that the way you and I treat our elders now will be the same way we are treated in our old age.

Geshe Michael Roche, author of *The Diamond Cutter*, says that if you want to heal loneliness and create a richer love, not to mention some great karma later in life: don't try to meet people at bars and clubs. Rather, go to an old age home, where you can sow seeds of love that will be instantly treasured.

There are so many "Robertas" out there, who led a great life, a successful life, and their older age became much more difficult than they ever imagined it to be. And they are suffering an oppressive loneliness for which your attention will be their greatest and rarest resource.

That night in New York City, we surrounded this lonely woman, fighting battles with health and money and love. But those are not her battles to fight alone. We all are trying to figure out health and money and love. Whatever loneliness anyone brought to that moment dissipated in the face-to-face, heart-to-heart, generation-to-generation *contact*.

Someone asked, "Roberta, can you turn the tide on your life? How does this get better for you?"

Roberta said, "People keep telling me how strong I am. I don't think so. I accept it. I'm not scared to die. Once it's over, it's over. I won't be in pain. I won't be worried about money."

I asked if she believes in life after death.

She replied, "I don't believe in anything except 'us.'"

"My stepdad, Harry Nye, who passed on at age 82 . . . was a quiet, humble, loving man. I learned so much from him being his authentic self. He was introverted, so I learned it was okay to not be a social butterfly. He asked my political opinions, so even as a young girl, I learned to speak and know my own truth. He raised me and my two brothers, so I learned integrity and how to be a stepparent—never trying to replace a parent, but being an additional adult to care about and care for a stepchild. He was not perfect and damn if I haven't learned that is okay too, and to keep on trying anyway."

—Lorri, Redmond, Washington

11

"SCREW," LAUGH, CELEBRATE (even at funerals)

God is a comedian playing to an audience too afraid to laugh.
—*Voltaire*

What could be more exciting than a trip to see the dermatologist?

On my last visit, the dermatologist blowtorched my forehead with dry ice, knifed a skin tag off my shoulder which both my children at a very young age had confused with a piece of candy, and shot a numbing agent into my back before excavating three chunks of flesh with a medical drill.

Oh, the joy!

I honestly think a morning run in Caracas or the northern territories of Afghanistan might be more joyful than a trip to the dermatologist.

But there was a saving grace. After a forty-five-minute drive to the dermatology office, I checked in with the receptionist.

I handed her my insurance card and asked, "I should have double-checked that you take my insurance. Do you take this?"

She looked at my card and studied it for ten long seconds. Then she said, "Actually we don't take this insurance."

It was like that slow motion moment in a Rocky movie when the villainous foe punches Rocky in the face and he spins around and around and everything gets blurry and you hear a drawn out *"Adrian!"* as Rocky collapses to the ground.

Are you freakin' serious? I was going to need to turn around and drive all the way home, having wasted 90 minutes of my day. As the F-bombs were seconds from exploding through my vocal cords . . .

"Just kidding," said the receptionist.

You usually don't experience humor in a doctor's office.

Bless her soul! I laughed so hard and it completely altered my mood and made the doctor's slicing, injecting, carving, and blowtorching a little less terrible.

If only the doctor could prescribe "Rx: three sidesplitting, tear-jerking laughs. 1 in the morning, 1 after lunch, 1 before dinner."

When is the last time you had such a laugh? I recently went to a comedy club in New York City. A few of the comedians were so funny that tears were running down my face. Snot was dripping from my nose. I even farted, out loud, I lost control and it was exhilarating!

Sometimes I forget that humor is the most healing medicine, the most accessible medicine, and the most forgotten medicine. Humor is one thing from a receptionist or a comedian. But an elder who has felt pain, and more pain, and even more pain, and is still laughing—I want to laugh with that person.

That person is Lorena.

Lorena, 83 years old, showed up late to a Drinks with Your Elders event in Dallas. She looked around at the audience, a mix of men and women from 20-50 years old. Lorena asked, "Where are the widows?"

"The widows?"

"Yes, I'm here to speak to the widows."

"This event is called Drinks with Your Elders. We are here to hear your story."

She thought she was coming to a speak at a widow support group rather than to a bunch of young people drinking wine. But Lorena rolled with it. That's what she does. She rolls with it.

In the early 1980s, Lorena was happily married. She had two children. Then she was hit by a wave of pain and struggle. In 1981, she was told she had breast cancer, and she had six months to live.

She persevered. "I'm still here today. If you have your health, you can choose whether to be happy or sad."

Then her husband was diagnosed with ALS and passed away in 1983. "We were blessed. It was fast."

Over the next few years, Lorena suffered nine deaths of close relatives. She said, "The Lord held my hand the whole time. I kept talking to him and he said 'You again?'"

I asked how all the death changed her.

"I appreciated life more. Before, I took so much for granted. And I was young. Everything was new. I was learning to be a good mom, a good wife. Now with the grandchildren and great-grandchildren, I appreciate them more."

She got married again in 1996. "My second husband was retired, and he had two boys who I called my bonus children.

He was full of fun and laughter. He was not a stranger to anybody. We were a match. Our spirits were the same in that if you can make someone smile, just one smile, it will reward you forever because it just makes you feel good."

Then her second husband died of a heart attack.

Lorena said of the sad days to follow, "I was floating but I didn't know where I was. I just said 'yes' to everything."

To anyone going through a hard time, Lorena advises, "Even though hurt comes, eventually you will find something good from that. It's hard to believe that old saying, 'The sun will shine again' but I truly believe it. It's hard to find something good out of something bad."

The audience at the Drinks with Your Elders event was feeling her pain. The room was silent. People stopped sipping their wine and sat with heavy hearts.

We got a lot from Lorena's courage, which would have been more than enough.

But then, Lorena worked her magic and told a story.

"On the evening before a memorial service, I was with my family. Everyone was together and fooling around. My sister's 19-year-old, 6'2" grandson was on the floor playing. He didn't see me and clipped me on the knees. I flew backward and broke my femur bone. They put a rod in there and some screws."

And with a straight face, she said, "I was screwed by rod, and I didn't like it."

She pierced the weight of the moment and had the audience at the Drinks with Your Elders event in hysterics.

Lorena said, "It's a hard world to live in. You have to laugh in life."

There's always something causing pain. Your back hurts. You got in an argument with your boss. Your kids aren't doing their homework. And it's making you crazy!

Buddhist monk Thich Nhat Hanh said, "Sometimes joy is the source of your smile. But sometimes a smile is the source of your joy."

In other words, fake it 'til you make it.

As Lorena finished her story that night in Dallas, we lifted our wine glasses high in the air.

"To life."

"To love."

"To laughter."

"My mother, Betty Deering, lived to be 83 years old. She gave so much of her time listening to people. I always wondered how she could drop anything at a moment's notice and be there for anyone, anytime. She listened to my stories as if I were the most important person in the universe. She never gave me answers without leading me to find them myself. It was my mom who taught me that to listen to others is the best gift you can ever offer another human being. To validate another in such a way that they matter and that time is a treasure beyond anything you can ever give as a gift. I am now a listener. The gift is in the receiving . . . the knowledge, wisdom, tears, and laughter, stories, history, sharing, enjoying anyone and everything. Thank you, mama, for teaching me as I am now teaching my own children. As teenagers now they are old souls—, empowered by history books, humbled by their third world experiences, excited to sit with elders, kids, anyone, and hear stories without being consumed by their phones or themselves. I am so proud that they are the next generations of listeners."

—Becky, Anchorage, Alaska

12

RAISE KIDS WHO WANT TO SPEND TIME WITH YOU (even when they're all grown up)

If you think their messy room is hard to look at, just wait until it's empty.

—*Anonymous mom*

A cruise ship docked in a tiny Greek village. An American tourist got off the boat, ventured into the village, and saw a Greek fisherman. He complimented the Greek fisherman on the quality of his fish and asked how long it took him to catch them.

"Not very long," answered the Greek.

"But then, why didn't you stay out longer and catch more?" asked the American.

The Greek explained that his small catch was sufficient to meet his needs and those of his family.

The American asked, "But what do you do with the rest of your time?"

"I sleep late, fish a little, play with my children, and take a siesta with my wife. In the evenings I go into the village to see my friends, dance a little, drink a bit, and sing a few songs. I have a full life."

The American interrupted, "I have an MBA from Harvard and I can help you. You should start by fishing longer every day. You can then sell the extra fish you catch. With the revenue, you can buy a bigger boat.

"With the extra money the larger boat will bring, you can buy a second one and a third one and so on until you have an entire fleet of trawlers. Instead of selling your fish to a middleman, you can negotiate directly with the processing plants and maybe even open your own plant.

"You can then leave this little village and move to Athens, London, or even New York City! From there you can direct your huge enterprise."

"How long would that take?" asked the Greek.

"With the power of the internet and if you make the right hires, this can happen quickly—a few years," replied the American.

"And, after that?"

"That's when it gets really interesting," answered the American, laughing. "When your business gets really big, you can go public and make millions!"

"Millions? Really? And after that?"

"After that you'll be able to retire, live in a tiny village near the coast, sleep late, play with your grandchildren, catch a few fish, take a siesta with your wife, and spend your evenings singing, dancing, playing, and drinking with your friends . . ."

It's called the Western Circumstance. We spend all our health to gain our wealth, and then we must spend all our wealth to regain our health.

How do you bust loose from this vicious cycle?

Take a moment to examine your definition of the word "accomplishment."

◆   ◆   ◆   ◆

Florence, 82, told me right away that she has nothing extraordinary to share about her life. She called it "kind of dull."

Divorced since 1971, she raised three children as a single mom. There's nothing dull about being a single mom!

Her kids are now 60, 57, and 55, and they love spending time with their mother.

Florence described an ordinary life with jobs ranging from working the old dinosaur computers to waitressing. Whatever it took to care for her family. She was not the kind of person to whom the aforementioned Harvard businessman would pay much attention.

But then, she described a spark of something extraordinary. She called it a "magic spell with kids."

"My ex-husband and I say to our now adult children, 'We don't understand why you like us.' Our marriage was so horrible. For ten years we lived in misery. But we have such nice kids. They are very loving and affectionate. They work hard. They're good people. They love us and money can't buy that."

Both of Florence's sons broke high school sports records, even though their dad never threw them the ball. And Florence couldn't go to their games or practices because she had to work. But she made sure they had the right shoes, clean uniforms, everything they needed.

She said, "You can show your kids you care without being at the game."

Florence often worked the late shift as a waitress. She'd come home at 2:00 a.m., send her mom home, and go into her kids' rooms to make sure they were snug in bed. She would rub their backs and run her hands through their hair—for two hours at a time. She loved them as much as she could, whenever she could.

That kind of commitment when the money was tight, and the free time was tighter, creates the ultimate accomplishment in your older age: kids who love you and show up for you.

Florence's secret: "Don't cut your kids off when they're talking. Listen to everything they have to say. Sometimes it drags on, but listen."

It's an easy excuse to be too tired to listen. And that's when we are most susceptible to the Harvard businessman and his Western Circumstance. With all the numbers and charts in the world, you can never account for love.

When you are young, "accomplishments" are what you have to show for yourself. When you are older, "accomplishments" are the people showing up for you.

Note to self: Bust loose from the vicious cycle.

Run your hands through their hair.

Listen carefully to their words.

Love as best you can, when you can.

"In 2005, I had a newborn son pass away. I was miserable. I was low. My father, Charles, said to me in a whisper during the funeral, 'It's going to be okay.' In 2006, a short fifteen months later, I repeated those words to my dying father who was scared. In my lowest, weakest moments, I repeat those words to myself . . . sometimes in a whisper, sometimes in a scream. I tell it to my kids *all* the time."

—Autumn

13

BOUNCE BACK

You must face annihilation over and over again to find what is indestructible in yourself.

—*Pema Chodron, Buddhist teacher*

I lived in New York City for five years. Upon arrival in 2011, I was curious and ready to explore the sights and sounds of the Big Apple. Fast forward to 2016. I turned into the guy in the apartment building frantically knocking on everyone's door trying to figure out who was blowing pot smoke in the vents!

The noise and congestion of NYC took a toll on my sanity. And then, one weathered and wise New Yorker instilled in me some serious toughness.

I met Frouma, 90, at her Upper East Side apartment on a rainy summer day in 2015. She answered the door hobbling, in a nightgown. She had a thick Israeli accent, which is a kind of accent that always has an undertone that suggests, "Don't mess with me."

Frouma grew up in the part of Palestine that would one day become Israel. At five years old, she fell ill with polio and was paralyzed from toe to tongue. It took one year before it went away.

She said, "I would not give up. It took a long time. But hope was my weapon."

In her teens, Frouma began training with the Haganah, the underground Jewish paramilitary organization during Britain's occupation of Palestine. In Israel's War of Independence in 1948, Frouma fought on the front line at Gush Etzion. She was wounded, captured, and taken prisoner by the Jordanians who held her as a prisoner of war for five months. Without medical treatment and suffering from extreme thirst and hunger, Frouma almost died.

She described her survival as a "miracle."

"The heat killed the microbes and none of my fellow POW's even got infections from their wounds."

Frouma reiterated, "Hope is very powerful weapon. Never, ever give up hope."

During the bleakest moments, Frouma and her fellow POWs would whisper to each other, "Look at the light. Look at the light."

She carried that spirit into a 50-year career as a teacher of Judaic studies in the United States. She was honored for her dedication by senators and congressmen. She even had a letter from President George W. Bush honoring her many years of service as a teacher.

A few years after my initial meeting with Frouma, I called to say hello and reconnect. She said, "I want to tell you something. How many hearts do you have?"

I answered, "One heart."

She said, "Well, I have two hearts. My last name is Lev. Lev in Hebrew means heart. Whatever I say, I mean it with two hearts. I wish you the very best with all my heart(s)!"

That's the formula for resilience. Great toughness and greater love!

Jesuit priest Gregory Boyle writes, "Resilience is born by grounding yourself in your own loveliness, hitting notes you thought were way out of your range."

Rose Lindenberg, 94, knows these "notes" well.

Rose grew up in in the 1920s, living a comfortable family life in the Rhineland, a beautiful part of Germany. Her parents made a nice living. Life was good.

When Hitler came to power in 1933, all hell broke loose. As Rose recalled, "We knew Hitler was bad but we didn't know how murderous he and the Nazis really were."

Her father and brother were suddenly pulled out of their home by the Gestapo. Her father died in a concentration camp. Her brother escaped to Siberia.

Rose stayed with her mother in Germany only to witness Kristallnacht, the wave of violent anti-Jewish pogroms which took place in November 1938.

"That was the end. We had no family. No nations would take us. All the borders were closed. My mother saw that we wouldn't get out alive."

She had heard of a woman snuggling girls out of Germany and into Belgium. So at 14 years old, Rose saw her mother for the last time and was smuggled across the border. She doesn't know how her mother died, most likely in a concentration camp.

Just like that, her family was gone.

"It was the most traumatic thing. Somebody pulled the rug from under your feet. You don't know who you are. You are a stranger to everybody. I remember that feeling. It was horrible."

Rose was then part of the Kindertransport, the informal name of a series of rescue efforts which brought thousands of refugee Jewish children to Great Britain.

She arrived in London just a few days before the bombing blitz of London by the Nazis. The bombs killed over 50,000 and maimed 250,000 people. Rose survived. On top of the fact that the Nazis killed 1.5 million children, Rose considers it a miracle she is here today.

She didn't talk about her story for years and years but now in her 90s, she realizes how important it is to share it.

"I am still a witness," she said.

Rose considers herself the luckiest person in the world. She had no family when she came to America after the war, but she started fresh, got married, had two children, four grandchildren, and five great-grandchildren.

Rose's advice to young people. "With my own family, I hear them talking that they have issues. I will say, 'You don't even know what an issue is.'"

"I always have to believe better days are coming..."

◆ ◆ ◆ ◆

These stories about the atrocity of war remind us that the human spirit is powerful, that our elders endured and suffered, and, God forbid you ever need to dig that deep, you have what it takes.

At the moment I write this, my stepmom is the hospital, recovering from a traumatic accident. When you read "stepmom," it may not pull at your heartstrings like "mom" or "grandma." But she is a great source of love and light for our family and all who know her. She recently fell and sustained ten broken ribs. She was in intensive care and enduring the worst pain.

There was a period of several hours where our family was completely uncertain of her fate. In that bleak space of just waiting and praying and hoping and pacing, I thought about Frouma and Rose and the many stories of resilience I've heard from the elder generation.

Corinne, 92, and Barbara, 88, were guests at the Drinks with Your Elders in Chicago.

Corinne lost her husband to a heart attack in his early 40s. Suddenly a single mom with five children to raise, she said the family drew very close and developed a system. "I was tough. We had rules. Everybody worked and everybody contributed. And through it all, I always let my kids now how much I loved them, no matter what!"

Barbara lost both her parents to tuberculosis at a very young age. She and her three siblings were placed in an orphanage. Barbara made a very conscious decision to have a good attitude about the situation. Her siblings struggled, but Barbara developed an inner strength that stuck with her throughout life. She always knew she could and would rise above challenges.

Frouma, Rose, Corinne, and Barbara were all knocked down and had to find their way through the darkest moments. But love regenerated in their lives. They all had uplifting stories to share about the years after their pain and struggle.

In our darkest moments, may we remember the words and voices of our elders.

"Look at the light."

"Better days are coming."

"Always let your kids know how much you love them, no matter what!"

"Hope is a very powerful weapon. Never give up hope."

"My most memorable elder was a World War II pilot who flew a medical evacuation plane in Iwo Jima. I asked him if he shared his experiences with his children, grandchildren, etc. He said no. He didn't think they would be interested. I said he **was** a hero, thanked him for his service, and suggested he share his stories with his family. I met him at a golf outing—he'd volunteered and was serving us all cheese curds! I thought we should be serving him the cheese curds . . . he smiled. I have no idea what his name is. The life lesson: you never know who you will meet, but if you ask a few questions and listen, you just might be in the presence of someone very special."

—Andy, Madison, Wisconsin

14

SOOTHE THE PAIN

When each day is the same as the next, it's because people fail to recognize the good things that happen in their lives every day that the sun rises.

—*Paulo Coelho*

Surely you've been "pocket dialed." But what do you call it when your two-year-old gets his little hands on your phone and starts dialing?

I call it Dottie-Dialing.

Every time my son got a hold of my phone, he would unknowingly (or maybe knowingly) call the same person, listed in my phone as: "Dottie Hart-Drinks With Your Elders-Dallas."

Dottie was a featured elder at the Drinks with Your Elders event in Dallas in 2016.

I'd quickly hang up the call and take the phone away from my son. But Dottie would always call back.

I'd answer, "Hey Dottie. I'm so sorry, that was my two year-old calling you . . . again."

It didn't bother Dottie. She'd say in her East Texas twang, "Honey, I'm provin' that you can't die of boredom."

Translation: I'm lonely and it's good to hear from someone.

The first time I met Dottie, I knew there was something I liked, something catchy in her voice, her accent, her little quips. Did I mention her East Texas twang?

When I asked, "How are you?" she said, "Fair to middlin'."

"How's your health?"

She answered, "I'm on no medication. But there are no pills for orneriness. Hey, I got a joke for ya. A man called his wife and said, 'I just killed five flies. Three are male and two are female.' The wife said, 'How do you know which are which?' The man said, 'I killed three of them on beer cans and two of them on the phone.'"

Dottie is "an original cow girl." She grew up on a 140-acre ranch in East Texas with 100 white-faced Hereford cattle. She loved her daddy. He was a war hero who fought in the 13th armored division under Patton in World War II. Dottie recalled visiting him in the hospital, where his arm was amputated, and he spent months recovering after the war.

Her dad became constable of their hometown, Belton, Texas (population 8,000). He didn't allow Dottie to date soldiers "for fear I'd fall in love and marry one and end up in Timbuktu."

Dottie recalled, "I was Daddy's girl from day one. I sat on his lap when I was like twenty-one and home from nursing school."

Her parents were killed in a car accident in 1962.

"They had to use the Jaws of Life to get Daddy out and Mommy flew out the windshield. They didn't have seat belts then."

"Even though I'd been around death and dying in nursing, the loss of my parents was a shocker. I decided the things I had been taking for granted, like tomorrow, you can't do that. Today is all you got promised. I'm thankful for every day I have."

Dottie fondly remembered her dad walking around the house and strumming the guitar, playing country songs by Hank Williams, Roy Acuff, and Johnny Cash.

"Country" is her thing. There's "country" in her voice, her stories, her memories, her jokes. It's something simple but profound. Harlan Howard famously said, "Country music is three chords and the truth."

I sometimes long for that simpler, easier life. Don't you?

Life always has something coming down the pike. Health. Bills. Taxes. Throw in a death, divorce, a move, and you are busting at the seams. What a great moment for the soothing simplicity of country music (and Dottie-dialing).

I'd never cared much for country music. Then I went to college in Nashville and developed an appreciation for the relatable stories and feel-good livin' they sing about in country songs.

Cold beer on a Friday night.

Barefoot on the warm sand.

A heart full of gratitude for the ones you love.

On the bad days, the long weeks, the painful months when we are hemorrhaging trust and hope, we need those moments to slow down and tip life back in our favor.

On April 28, 2018, when that car hit my daughter in the stroller, I remember being in the backyard with my kids. Several hours had passed since the hit-and-run incident. My daughter, only sixteen months at the time, waddled around in her diaper, chased by her brother.

My mind was tipping back and forth, at one second filled with gratitude that my children are healthy—and the next second, distraught at what transpired a few hours earlier.

A new "country" song, *Living*, came on the radio.

Dierks Bentley sang,

Some days you just breathe in
Just try to break even

Sometimes your heart's poundin' out of your chest
Sometimes it's just beating

Some days you just forget
What all you've been given

Some days you just get by
Some days you're just alive
Some days you're livin'

It described how I felt leading up to that moment. I'd been breaking even, forgetting what I've been given, taking too much for granted. Here I have these beautiful children and a beautiful wife but I wanted more. I needed more.

After what went down with my daughter, "my heart was pounding out of my chest" and I wanted to dig in and appreciate these moments with my family.

I'm talking about the moments before bath and bedtime when it's tempting to cut corners and get to the end of the day a little faster. I'm talking about the moments when my son wants one more bedtime story so he can drag it out and stay awake as late as possible. I'm talking about the moments when my daughter needs another diaper change because she is teething and I can't find the diaper cream for her diaper rash and it's the tenth diaper of the day. There are a lot of these moments when I'm feeling like a tired 45-year-old dad with high-energy children.

An older father with grown kids once told me, "I know you're tired right now raising little kids. You worry about money and stuff like that. But trust me, enjoy this time in your life. I see my kids a few times each year, if I'm lucky. They're busy and all grown up. So I have all the freedom in the world but it's nothing compared to the time when your kids are little and you have all the love in the world. I'd take love over freedom any day, anytime.'"

I thought of that wisdom, "love over freedom any day, anytime," as that country song was playing and my kids were running on our little patch of grass in the backyard.

On that same patch of grass, a few days later, I found a pile of feathers. I had never found a single feather in my backyard. And here there were eight of them. I'd heard there is a symbolism to feathers. It means "protection" or "the angels are near." Many people suggested that angels protected my daughter in that hit-and-run.

I saved those feathers and framed them and not a day goes by where I don't see them.

A college buddy said to me, "Feathers? Those are from a dead bird. Disgusting. Why would you frame them? Throw them away!"

But when I fall back into busy days and ungrateful ways, I look to those feathers and think of that wisdom and listen to that country song. It's a lot more fun to believe, than not to believe.

This philosophy won't solve your problems nor pay your bills. But it will give you some perspective.

As Dottie said, "Sometimes you just gotta lasso a star and climb up to it."

"My Grandmother, Dolores, lived to the age of 92 and was my favorite coffee buddy during my twenties and thirties. She was a model of love and acceptance and I remember her living her life by 'The Book.' I cherished our coffee dates and listening to her compare life in the present and past. I remember one day I went to visit my Grandma. It was not to have coffee but to share the news that I was pregnant. She was aware that I was recently divorced and single, so I was quite nervous about how my grandmother, a born-again Christian, would take the news. Well, she listened with love and acceptance and she saw the look of shame on my face and said, 'My dear, I love you and you are not unique. You are not the first person in this family who is in this situation and you probably won't be the last.' Then she went on to share the story of how she had to ditch my mother's deadbeat father (her first husband) with three children and another one on the way. She soon fell in love with her second husband, our grandpa, who she was married to for seventy years. She was outcast from her church and the people in the small Texan town where she lived—but she trusted herself. She let me know that she trusted me and my decisions too. What a great friend!"

—Tricia, Milpitas, California

15

HOW TO DIE
(and keep living)

We are all travelers in the wilderness of this world, and the best we can find in our travels is an honest friend.
—*Robert Louis Stevenson*

Is there life after death?

Why waste time wondering when you can hear firsthand from a "witness."

A mutual friend told me, "You have to meet my friend Jackie. She died once for twenty minutes which really changed her attitude and seemed to reset her clock! Amazingly youthful."

Her friend was spot on.

Jackie and I met at a loud cafe in Los Angeles.

Even through the chaos, Jackie's presence soothed. She appears very young, not just in the way of skin and tone. Her energy is vibrant. She has lucid blue eyes and a calming voice that was somewhat faint and hard to hear in the loud restaurant.

I leaned in and listened to every word as Jackie shared her story of vacationing with three friends in Egypt in 1995.

Before she departed, she'd been having asthmatic conditions and this trip to Egypt made her four children very nervous. But spiritual author and teacher Marianne Williamson was leading part of the tour and Jackie insisted on being there! So she loaded up on prednisone for her asthma and off she went.

While touring the pyramids, Jackie didn't realize they had to take a horse and buggy. She is allergic to horses, but figured she could get through it.

Jackie remembers struggling to breathe. The tour operators gave her oxygen but it wasn't helping. She was going into anaphylactic shock.

Her last thoughts were, "I knew I was dying. I came to Egypt to die. My kids are going to be so unhappy with me. That's the last thing I remember and then I let go.

"I floated through a gray tunnel. It was all love, explosions of love. Other peoples' near-death experiences may vary but the love is all the same. It's a love you can't describe."

"[During this near-death experience] I was taken to an outdoor temple and laid on a flat stone. There were beings in brown capes and hoods. I couldn't see their faces. They were all coming up the hill, praying, chanting, and surrounding me. And it was just beautiful music and explosions of love."

Meanwhile, the lady who ran the Egyptian tour was a former emergency room nurse. Frantically performing CPR, she and Jackie were rushed to the clinic. The doctor said there was nothing he could do. Jackie's eyes were fixed and open. Her tongue was blue. She was gone.

But the former ER nurse refused to give up.

Jackie said, "I could feel the bottom half of my body moving and this male voice said, 'She's alright, she is having contractions.'"

And finally, miraculously, Jackie inhaled.

When she came to, she was told that her heart had stopped for twenty minutes. Her friend describes her as "a scientific anomaly."

Later that night, Jackie was carried back to the cruise ship. Her fellow passengers had heard she was dead so you can imagine their shock to see her alive! They applauded her and some even asked for her autograph.

What a day.

Jackie said, "Before I came back to life, this male voice repeated to me over and over, 'Just remember, all that matters is love.' I wasn't sure what do that with message."

She is still processing it, twenty-three years after her near-death experience.

Jackie's son died of an overdose in 2006. She recalled her anger and frustration with him. She was working hard to pay the bills and here was her 45-year-old son, living at her house and sleeping late into the day.

She wished she would have handled it differently. Looking back, "He already felt like a failure. But everything I said reinforced that. So I would not have attacked him. I would have let him know how much I love him and how concerned I was for him."

To anyone with a difficult relationship, Jackie advises, "Through the anger and the frustration, make sure they know how much you love them."

That message "all that matters is love" has also taught her to be a more honest person.

"Honesty is love."

Her five grandchildren come to Jackie for advice because they appreciate her honesty. Maybe it comes from her near-death experience. Maybe it is just her personality. But she holds a light that draws you near.

When I returned to the recording of my conversation with Jackie, I heard myself sharing details with her about my personal life. I didn't know her at all, but I revealed so much about myself. That is the thing about her light, her honesty. It made me want to take off and let go of anything that stood between myself and her light.

God forbid it takes a near-death experience to help us shed the layers and speak, think, and live more honestly.

But it very well may take some sort of danger to awaken.

❖　❖　❖　❖

I woke up one morning in December 2017 and the fire index was 296, the highest it has ever been, according to the Los Angeles Fire Chief.

The winds were blowing strong, in some places 60 or 70 mph. The smoky air burned your eyes. My son was coughing. The 405 Freeway, which Los Angelenos drive most every day of their lives, was surrounded by smoldering hills. It felt like a nuclear winter with ash falling and the skies a soupy gray.

The wailing sirens never seemed to end, which made it hard to sleep.

I woke up at 3:30 a.m. and walked outside, not knowing what to expect. The strong Santa Ana winds fueling the fires actually cleared the sky over my house.

And for the first time in my forty-five years, I looked up and saw a meteor shower, or stars falling across the skies of metropolitan Los Angeles.

Fire burned, smoked billowed, but through it all, there was an opening in the skies . . . and falling stars! It's so true what they say: the same wind that carries crisis, also carries opportunity.

Never has my city, and the whole world for that matter, felt so vulnerable and so dangerous. On my drive to meet Jackie, there was an earthquake. Literally, the earth shook as I drove down the offramp.

But when I met with her, I felt something like a clearing amidst the danger. I now interpret that clearing as "honesty." It took Jackie dying for twenty minutes to understand its value.

As Warren Buffet said, "Honesty is a very expensive gift. Do not expect it from cheap people."

Only 5 percent of Americans have reported a near-death experience. Most people don't have direct exposure to the light. Jackie's pure sense of honesty is rare.

My closest brush with honesty on a regular basis is with a friend who tells you how he sees it.

When you have a pimple, he's the guy who will flat out say to you, "What's wrong with your skin?" When you are a little overweight, he won't beat around the bush, "You look like a pig."

And that was before he went to Tony Robbins.

Now he asks for permission. But if you give it to him, he will eviscerate you and every bad decision you are making and every stupid thing you ever said and every habit that is holding you back. He is a tornado of wisdom, power, and intense criticism. In the moment, it is a lot to handle.

But looking back, *God bless him*! God bless everyone who has the courage to be honest. Because too many people, myself included, go through life comfortable in the darkness.

Marianne Williamson famously said, "Our deepest fear is that we are powerful beyond measure. It is our Light, not our Darkness, that most frightens us."

More often than not, it takes something extreme to awaken us to our Light. A breakup, an illness, a near-death experience.

But there is an easier way.

Ask your most honest friend this very simple question: What am I not seeing about my career, my relationship, my life?

Their answer may stop your heart for a moment or two. But as Jackie would attest, you'll come back younger, stronger, and with a far greater capacity for love, light, truth . . . all the good stuff!

"I remember my Dedo (which means 'grandfather' in Macedonian) being the life of the party. He always had a quick wit, a little hip shake, a jab with the finger. 'Hey-hey' he'd say to people he connected with. He kind of felt like a cross between Frank Sinatra and Sammy Davis Jr. He wore bright colorful clothes and big brimmed hats. He called his good guy friends 'baby,' and he just was cool. He had a big spirit, and I just felt good all the time when I was around him. I felt like celebrating. He was a musician. He played the clarinet and the trumpet. One time he told me a story about how he got to play with Duke Ellington. Duke and his crew were cruising through town playing at a road stand outside of Fort Wayne, Indiana. His dad told him about it. So he hitched a ride on the back of a pickup truck with his trumpet in hand and headed to the show. He was one of the pickup players that Duke selected to play with him that night. I learned from this story that you always got to take your chance when it's right in front of you—find a way to get into the light and it will shine on you. My grandfather was only fifteen years old when he got the chance to sit in the company of Duke Ellington. The Duke went on to be one of the biggest big band musicians in the country. Show up and take a chance. That's what I learned from him."

—Katrina, Chicago, Illinois

16

MAKE A MASSIVE IMPACT

Often we are caught in a mental trap of seeing enormously successful people and thinking they are where they are because they have some special gift. Yet a closer look shows that the greatest gift that extraordinarily successful people have over the average person is their ability to get themselves to take action.

—Tony Robbins

Earlier this year, I signed up for a training in Transcendental Meditation, otherwise known as TM. You've probably heard about the guru Maharishi Mahesh Yogi who taught TM to the Beatles in the 1960s. Much of the Beatles' "White Album" was inspired by their time spent in India with Maharishi.

So many people swear by the power of TM to soothe the mind, improve sleep, concentrate, regulate stress. I had to try . . .

I was told to show up for the first day of TM training with a piece of fruit, a white handkerchief, and a bouquet of flowers. Not to mention, it costs hundreds of dollars. At first, it felt a little cultish and over-the-top spiritual.

On day 1 of the training, my TM teacher gave me my mantra, taught me about the TM technique, and led me through a meditation. After one hour, the first day of training was complete. I felt nice, but . . .

I said to the teacher, "I thought for the money I paid, we would have done more today."

In a very peaceful tone, the teacher put me in my place. "Listen, when you get on a plane to go somewhere, you don't need to know how the plane works, what the pilot is doing in the cockpit, what kind of fuel the plane uses. You just sit in your seat, watch your movie, relax, and the plane gets you there.

"When you send an email, you don't need to know how your computer breaks down the data and sends it across cyberspace. You just press 'send' and trust that the email will arrive on the other person's computer.

"So it is with the TM technique. Just do the technique. Your mind will relax. It's the easiest thing in the world."

He was right. It is the easiest thing in the world. I do TM every day. It works. There's nothing spiritual about it.

In moments when I overthink life, worry too much, create fake stories in my mind, I remember the advice of the TM teacher, "You just sit in your seat and the plane gets you there;" "You just press send and the email arrives."

In other words, why waste your life thinking about the stuff you don't need to think about?

Get yourself into action.

It's the same practical, no-nonsense approach that Barry Segal, 83, uses to change the world, every single day.

Barry started out working in his family business. He married his girlfriend during his sophomore year in college. They had five kids and at thirty-one, Barry branched out and started his own company distributing roofing materials. It began to grow, and Barry continued opening branches, until his operation reached 150 branches and nearly $2 billion in sales. Barry sold the business in 2007.

After selling his business, he went to the Clinton Global Initiative. He met a woman from South Africa, Anne, starting a project in Rwanda much like a kibbutz, or cooperative community. Barry and his wife went on a trip with Anne in Africa and decided to fund their project. That was just the beginning.

Barry then saw an article in *Sports Illustrated* about Kip Keino, the great Kenyan runner and Olympic champion. Keino turned his home in Kenya into an orphanage for 35 kids. Barry sent him a donation.

A short time later, Barry read an article about doctors working in Uganda. Barry sent them a donation.

He said, "We deal with a lot of people with very small budgets who do amazing stuff."

He then told me about an eye doctor who was going to Liberia to treat people. He gave her some money. Now, this doctor has a clinic in Liberia. As Barry said, "Those are the type of things we like to do."

Barry has always believed in the power of the individual to create change. But you have to take action. Action might be as simple as writing a letter. Barry recently assembled a massive binder of all the letters he has written throughout his life, like the one he wrote after his first wife died of cancer at 42 years old.

Barry was called for jury duty shortly after his wife died. While he sat, waiting to be called by the clerk, cigarette smoke polluted the air. The non-smoking laws were recently put into effect but they were not well enforced. Barry was disgusted and walked out of jury duty in protest.

Barry wrote a letter to the court explaining why he left, saying that the non-smoking law was not being enforced. Someone from the court system wrote back saying that he too had lost his wife to cancer, and they would be sure to enforce the smoking rules from that point forward. Barry's letter made a difference.

His binder of letters includes those penned to Bill Clinton, Bloomberg, and Obama. But Barry is not afraid to protest the old-fashioned way, one person, one picket sign, one voice at a time.

He said, "We see the wealthy get wealthier and the lower classes slipping. A lot of things don't make sense to me. In the northeast, if you have an EasyPass, you pay $10 for tolls. If you can't afford an EasyPass, you pay $15 for tolls. The poorer people lose."

A few years ago, when New York and New Jersey created this increase in the EasyPass toll fare, Barry made picket signs reading, "The Fares ain't Fair," and asked everyone from his office to picket with him outside the Holland Tunnel.

Each of us has this power to create an extraordinary impact. But you have to activate this power, by getting out of your head and taking a step into action.

In his book *What Is the Bible?* Rob Bell writes, "There are lots of reasons all around us every day to make us believe that we don't matter, that our choices aren't significant, that it's all just a meaningless slide into nothingness. The writers of the Bible speak against this, insisting that you can make choices to live in particular ways, that you can decide to use your voice and your energies for healing and building up, and that you can help take things in a different direction. In story after story in the Bible, the hero is flawed and frail, prone to make all kinds of mistakes, stumbling through life with a fairly pathetic batting average. In other words, the Bible is a library of books about people a lot like us, trying to figure it out, doing what they can to make a go of it."

In this sense, Barry is "biblical." When he first visited Africa in 2007, he noticed the conditions in the rural areas. There were six or seven children per mother. Many of the four- and five-year-old children carried a one-year-old on their backs. Mothers would sell children for cattle in arranged marriages. In some countries, the people had an average of a third grade education.

Barry took action.

He started the Segal Family Foundation and has funded over 200 NGOs (non-governmental organizations.) He said, "We like to take small, grassroots operations and see them grow. We'll give $10 or $15,000 dollars and more as time goes on. Before you know it, they'll have a budget of $700,000."

The Segal Family Foundation gives away approximately $1 million per month, much of it in sub-Saharan Africa. The foundation's successes have made it a major role model in the non-profit world. Leaders of African nations have met with the Segal Family Foundation to learn how to mobilize NGOs and get them to collaborate.

Now one could argue, "This guy Barry Segal is a man of extraordinary means. It's easy to make an impact when you rub elbows with the wealthy and powerful like the Clintons, Barbara Bush, and Robert Kennedy Jr."

Barry wasn't always rich. But he always believed he could make an impact.

When I finished my interview with Barry, I thought about all those times I wanted to write a letter to the airlines, to the credit card company, to the politician. I never end up writing the letters. I always assume it's a waste of time. Who would ever read my letter?

Occasionally I post something on social media that I feel strongly about. But I only have 5,000 followers. Is that really going to move the needle when people have 100,000 or 1,000,000 followers? Is it really worth posting?

That's not Barry Segal's schtick.

The Director of Pediatric Health Initiatives for his Focus for Health foundation, Sheri Marino, said, "Barry is passionate about making the world a better place. He often says, 'this just doesn't make sense' and then he'll go after it and won't give up."

I don't think he does TM. But he certainly is not beholden to an overactive, stressed out mind steeped in worry and fear. That's enemy number one to getting it done.

Whatever you feel strongly about, stop thinking so much. Write the letter. Make the call. Take the action.

"My grandfather Enrique was the absolute most loving man I've ever known. He passed away when I was 20 years old, on January 11, 2010, at 78. We had a bond no one else had. There was so much chaos in my family, within my immediate home life and within the rest of the family, but when I was with my Papa everything disappeared. We had a magical bubble that surrounded us and it was filled with love and light."

—Lucy, San Diego, California

17

HOW TO FIND MORE TIME

They say I'm old fashioned
and live in the past
Sometimes I think progress
Progresses too fast.
            —*Dr. Seuss*

According to a study by Censuswide and Reebok, the average life span is 25,915 days. The average human spends:

.45% (117 days) having sex
.69% (180 Days) exercising
6.8% (1,769 days) socializing with someone they love
41% (10,625 days) looking at a screen

How is all your screen time impacting your humanity?

Entire days go by where I'm so busy on my computer, the only people I talk to are immediate family. Human interaction is waning and when we actually make contact, it has to be quick.

Imagine if someone said to you, "Hey can you take 10 minutes to watch this video I made?"

Ten minutes? Are you serious?

This stacks the odds against engaging with our elders. The elders are often less adept at social media, and they talk in longer soundbites that require you to have patience—lots and lots of patience.

Paulo Coelho said, "The two hardest tests on the spiritual road are the patience to wait . . . and the courage not to be disappointed with what we encounter."

In the past, I would've failed those two tests almost every day.

Now, I am learning, slowly but surely, the secret to passing those tests. You can't be efficient and patient at the same time.

◆ ◆ ◆ ◆

A friend introduced me to her Aunt Addie, 93 years young. We connected on the phone and I asked Addie how old she feels.

"I still feel like forty on the inside."

She worked as a kindergarten assistant for thirty-two years.

"At 85, I was teaching kids how to go down the slide."

She cried the day she was told the school couldn't keep her any longer.

Addie explained to me, "I'm still young-acting. I walk every day. I ride a bike every day. I socialize. I travel. I am very alive and vibrant."

There was a time in life where she didn't have that kind of freedom. Addie had three children in two and a half years. I asked how she got through it.

"I cried a lot."

Addie met her late husband on a train. She proudly shares his picture to this day and says, "Isn't he handsome?"

And yet, with all her vitality and spunk, there was a moment of frustration for both Addie and me. At the end of our conversation, I asked her to email me a photo. She said, "I can send you a photo in the mail."

"Can you email it?" I reiterated. "The mail takes too long."

"I can write down your email and give it to one of my grandchildren. They will send you something."

"Okay, ready? Here's my email. Yeah dave at mac dot com," I said.

Addie muttered, "Wait a minute, what? 'X'?"

I slowed down and said, "No. 'Y', like the letter 'Y'."

"Okay 'Y'."

Then I said, "'E' like 'eat'."

She repeated, "Okay. 'Y.' 'E.'"

I continued, "Then 'A' like 'apple'."

"Okay."

"Then 'H' like 'hat'."

"Okay."

"'D' like 'David'."

She said, "Pardon. 'D?' I got 'Y' 'E' 'A' 'H'. Now a 'D'?"

I was starting to get a little frustrated.

I said, "Yes. Then an 'A' like 'apple'."

Addie asked, "Again? Another 'A'?"

"Yes. Then 'V' like 'victory'."

She affirmed, "I got 'Y' 'E' 'A' 'H' 'D'."

"Right, then 'A' like 'apple'."

"Again. Another 'A?'"

"Yes. Then 'V' like 'victory'."

Now it was getting painful.

I continued, "Then 'E' like 'eat.' So it's YEAHDAVE."

"Another 'E'?"

"Yes."

Addie asked, "Now are these all together or hyphenated or what?"

Anytime you spell out your email for someone and it takes more than 20 seconds, that's 20 seconds too long. It took another 30 seconds to explain the "at" or @ symbol.

"Then it's mac.com. So it's 'M' like mom. Then 'A' like apple."

She said, "Wait a minute. You gave me an A before."

And then I just started laughing.

She said, "What's so funny?"

I replied, "Email is just a generational thing."

She quipped, "I know. I'm an old fart."

We are fifty years apart in age, but in that moment, she felt like one of my very best friends. And I realized, the joke was on me, not her. I had this perception that taking three minutes to give someone my email could have been three minutes appropriated for something more useful.

Like what? Like looking at the Facebook post of my friend Kate's trip to Milan with her husband or reading about the missile strike in Syria and the demise of US/Russia relations and my Dodgers losing 9 of their first 14 and then getting back to perusing the ten promotional emails that hit my inbox since I started writing this chapter.

My generation is so focused on the fastest, most efficient way to get through the day. If you can do it on a screen, why bother leaving your desk. If you can learn about it in a short video, why bother watching a long one. But where is that getting us?

When you put your head on the pillow to sleep at night, what do you remember? What do you talk about? Is there a cherished moment from your day that you can share? Or did it all happen too fast and too efficiently to remember anything?

I had so much to share from my conversation with Addie, who reminded me that parenting has forever been challenging, and all the parents from all the generations had tough days and hard times and got through it. She spoke of staying engaged and challenged, teaching kindergarten until she was 93, doing her own shopping as long as she can, and making a choice to never to think of herself as old.

When I put my head on the pillow to go to sleep that night, I said to my wife, "Honey, today I spoke with a 93-year-old lady. It took me seven minutes to give her my email address and those were the best, funniest, and most memorable seven minutes I've had in a long, long time. And here's what Addie told me before we said goodbye . . .

"'Love is the best thing in the world.'"

"I have written down everything that my art teacher, Joe Krush, 100, has said. When I shared the list with him recently, he almost sadly said that most of it wasn't originally his, but things he had learned from others. I told him that I appreciated the fact that he cared enough to pass on what he had learned from others, and that he recognized the value of it. And that he knew enough to know it could make a difference to others as it had for him. What is often noted about Joe is his humility. He says he is a nobody. Of course we, his students, disagree. We appreciate what he has to say, because we know what we don't know, even though he says he wants to make us aware of what we *do* know. Funny how that goes."

—Gloria, Malvern, Pennsylvania

18

FEEL INSTANTLY SUCCESSFUL

There is only one success: To be able to spend your life in your own way.
—*Christopher Morley, American author*

Tim Ferriss once interviewed music producer Rick Rubin. He asked Rubin, "When you think of the word 'successful,' who is the first person who comes to mind?"

Rick Rubin is possibly the most famous music producer. He has worked with everyone in the industry. I was really curious to hear his answer.

There was a long silence and then Rubin said, "That's not such an easy question to answer. There are so many things that go into success."

"What are some of those things?" Ferriss asked.

"I would start with somebody who is happy. I know a great many people who are financially successful but not happy. So I would rule them out to start with."

Then Rubin referred to an 80-year-old "friend from the beach" who did twenty-three pull-ups on the beach the other day. He said that this 80-year-old retired in his 50s because he wanted to spend his days enjoying his life and exercising. He is one of the most successful people on so many levels.

Here's a guy, Rick Rubin, who produced Eminem, the Dixie Chicks, Metallica, Run DMC, LL Cool J. He has won eight Grammys. And he cites the most successful person as an 80-year-old from the beach.

I heard this podcast on a run and never caught the name of the 80-year old from the beach. But the image stuck with me. Instead of the dude driving the fancy sports car and working in the big office with two assistants and overseeing a team of employees, it is the dude enjoying the sunshine, the waves, the freedom.

I am forever aligned with, and in awe of, those badasses who dare to defy the classic definition of success. They inspire us to check our seductions, jealousies, and desires at the door. They challenge us to stop consuming everyone else's light and start shining our own. And they remind us how simple it is to become "successful," even if you haven't felt that way.

Bill, 96, is one such badass.

Stationed in Hawaii on the morning of December 7, 1941, Bill remembers the Japanese fighter planes descending.

"It was five to seven in the morning and the lieutenant came screaming around the corner, 'Get them guns in position! We're at war!'

"We were too busy to be scared. By the time we got wheels underneath the 90 millimeter guns, and got them set up, and went to the ammunition dump, it was all over. We never got a shot."

"I could see the Arizona and I never saw black smoke go up in the air that far in my life."

He said, "The Army made a man out of me."

But Bill was tough long before the army. Growing up near Akron, New York, a small town with two stores, a gas station, and lots of farms, he started working at twelve years old. By the time he was fourteen, he was plowing fields, six days a week, ten hours a day, making 10 cents a day.

"Back then, you could buy jeans for 98 cents and seven gallons of gas for one dollar."

After the war, he got married and had three children. His wife died in 2016 at 94. They were married for 69 years.

"Do you miss her?" I asked.

"Absolutely. There's nobody perfect. But she was a perfect mother and a perfect wife."

Bill had a career in trucking, then a stint at Chevrolet, and a final chapter as a porter at a car dealership. He only recently retired at 92.

Here's a man who never made more than $27,000 a year but still loves and values hard work.

"I was ready to punch in and go to work! God honors people who work. The Bible says, 'He that don't work don't eat.'"

Bill has a method to making work so joyful.

He sings.

Bill shared his favorite memory of being 16 and getting a new John Deere 4020 diesel tractor. "What a tractor that was! I'd be out there eight hours a day, no break, bottle of water, no ice in it. I loved to plow. I'd sing out there like a trooper.

Country songs. Nobody could hear me. I enjoyed every minute of it."

Nowadays, Bill is in a band called Just For Fun with seven, eight, sometimes ten people who play in nursing homes. Bill plays harmonica and sings country, bluegrass, and gospel songs.

I asked if he could play one for me. He started with the harmonica and then sang for me in a voice that was gorgeously haggard, if you can imagine:

> *"You are my sunshine*
> *My only sunshine*
> *You make me happy*
> *When skies are gray*
> *You'll never know, dear*
> *How much I love you*
> *Please don't take my sunshine away."*

I took Bill's advice and tried singing that very song, "You are My Sunshine." Of course, some people just do not want to hear you sing.

My three-year-old asked me to be quiet so he could concentrate on Peppa Pig on TV. But I'm certain some part of him was moved, if not emotionally, then away from me and toward the other side of the couch.

But that's the key. To keep moving, to keep singing—on your tractor, in your career, on your journey.

You have periods of movement and momentum, shifts that will carry you forward. You can feel things building. The breakthrough is coming. You've worked so hard for this moment. Here it comes . . . and then . . .

You get stuck.

Nothing changes.

The same patterns repeat themselves.

You worked really hard . . . for nothing!

Ever felt that way?

Whenever it comes to spreadsheets and business plans, I get stuck.

Since 2015, I have been developing a wellness experience called 18 Minutes.

Imagine a comfortable space to get off your feet, smell the lavender from France, listen to a guided mindfulness session, all while you are horizontal and cozy underneath a weighted gravity blanket. When it's over, you indulge in an array of exotic chocolates and delicious wine. It's about resting your body, recharging your mind, rejuvenating your senses, and restoring your humanity—in just 18 minutes. Sounds interesting, right?

Well, I kept stalling at the point in development when it's time to create the spreadsheets and show there is real business behind 18 Minutes. In fact, my stalling became such an issue that the two business partners I'd been working with on 18 Minutes no longer had the patience. They were frustrated. I was frustrated. Something wasn't right.

In March 2018, I was preparing to do a pop-up version of 18 Minutes at South by Southwest in Austin, Texas. What an incredible opportunity! What should have been excitement became worrying about the execution of the concept, and thinking of my former partners and their frustration, and wondering if I could actually pull this off.

I remembered the one and only time we tested the 18 Minutes experience. It was at a swanky members-only club in

Chicago with a sophisticated consultant. We asked ten sample customers to run through the 18 Minutes experience and share their feedback with the consultant.

During the test, my partners grew frustrated because my attention to detail left much to be desired. I thought the whole test was a disappointment.

Several days later, we heard from the consultant who received and organized the feedback from the ten sample customers. I expected negative feedback and for the whole thing to be a bust.

But in his summary, the consultant said something very interesting, "I don't know if people will remember the words or the comfy chairs or the branding . . . but they will remember the soothing voice and the exotic chocolate and that wonderful lavender. That's how 18 Minutes will take off and spread."

I knew this to be true! I'd been teaching Yoga + Chocolate workshops for years and years. I know that people forget the details. But they always remember heightened sensory experiences. The taste of the chocolate, the touch on their scalp, the scent of the lavender. Why did I doubt myself?

The 18 Minutes pop-up at South by Southwest helped people to relax and make the time and space to taste, smell, breathe, and enjoy life deeply. By that standard, it hit the mark!

When you get stuck in the details, come back to the song in your heart.

Helen Schucman's book *A Course in Miracles* says, "Not the whole song has stayed with you, but just a little wisp of melody. But you remember, from just this little part, how lovely was the song, how wonderful the setting where you heard it, and how you loved those who were there and listened with you. Listen, and see if you remember an ancient song you knew so long ago and held more dear than any melody you taught yourself to cherish since."

Where do you find that "wisp of melody?"

How do play with the raw emotions that really move people?

How do you get unstuck?

How do you define success?

Start by looking at the song in your heart.

All you gotta do is sing.

"My grandfather, Stan Carter, is 94, still alive, still dancing, still singing, even Facetiming. He is a passionate atheist. He believes religion and belief in something beyond this life, beyond our reality, gives us an excuse to not live fully and completely in the moment, in joy, in gratitude, and most importantly in connection to each other and with what is. He has made it his job to telephone every one of his great-grandchildren, grandchildren, and children as much as possible. He handwrites cards for each of our birthdays, long, thoughtful, beautifully penned, and sends them in the mail so they arrive perfectly on time. He truly danced and sang though life. I will never stop hearing his voice singing: 'Smile though your heart is breaking. Smile even though it's aching. Although a tear may be ever so near, smile through the fear and sorrow. Smile and maybe tomorrow, you'll find that life is still worthwhile, if you just smile.' I am so blessed to have been close to him my entire life and cannot wait for him to finally hold my ten-month-old daughter this summer."

—Sarah, Los Angeles, California

19

BE REMEMBERED FOREVER

No one is ever more him/herself than when they really laugh.
Their defenses are down . . . If a new idea slips in at that
moment, it has a chance to grow.

—*George Carlin*

I recently took a flight with a hilarious Southwest Airlines flight attendant making announcements:

"And in the highly unlikely event of a water landing, just think of the incredible story you'll be able to tell your grandchildren!"

"If you're traveling with a small child, what were you thinking? Put your mask on first and then help them with theirs. If you are traveling with multiple young children, assist the one with the most potential first and then work your way down."

Actually, it was the longest hour of my life, because containing my one-year-old on a plane is tricky. She wanted to eat the pretzels she found between the seats, and play on the ground, and rip up the seat pocket safety instructions, and pull on the hair of the passenger in front of us.

Looking forward in life, it's never about the humor. It's always about the mission and the ambition. Get me there. Get me home. Get my child to please behave. Get my company to profitability. Get my back better. Get me a lover.

But looking back on life . . . *thank god* for the people who made you laugh.

◆ ◆ ◆ ◆

Hilarious and verbose, Ed, 96, wracked my brain with 80 minutes of nonstop stories, jokes, heartwarming love, and mind-bending chatter.

In the very beginning of our conversation, Ed shared a story about his mother when she was pregnant in 1921. At the doctor's office, his mother was reading an article to his father about the population growth in China. She read a line out loud, "This article says every fifth child born in the world will be Chinese."

Ed was about to be their fifth child, a few months from being born, and his father was then convinced that Ed would be born Chinese.

I was unsure if Ed was joking, until he told me his secret to longevity: "I love to see people laugh."

During World War II, Ed was a cryptographer working on breaking Japanese codes and messages. He remembers hearing the bombs whistling through the air. He said you could hear the bombs in the distance, but you couldn't hear the bombs that were coming right toward you.

"We kept going from island to island in the South Pacific. We would dig a trench for a latrine. So before we moved on to the next island, I had an idea to make the latrine ahead of time and when we got to the next island, we'd already have a screened-in latrine that you could sit on."

So Ed constructed this latrine which included four holes. "Why should we just look at these holes? Let's decorate the holes." He designed the holes in the shape of a diamond, spade, heart, and club.

"Two days later, I got called in by the Sergeant. 'You're the guy who cut these holes out?'"

"Yes sir!"

"The Captain sat on the latrine shaped like a heart, and scratched his ass on your carving. He is livid!"

Ed zigged and zagged, talked and delighted in his life story.

"My parents had nine children and we picked up a cousin who lost his parents. So ten children. Only three left now. Nobody had a birthday in the same month. So we had cake once a month, guaranteed!

"Anyway, the GI Bill of Rights was the best thing this country ever did. When I got out of the military, we heard that for every month we served, we got a month of college for free. And we could pick any college we wanted."

He went to the University of Illinois and went on to become a college professor of industrial design. He taught for forty years.

I discovered Ed through one of his former students who persisted and insisted that I met his college Professor "Ed" Zagorski.

The student remembered:

"He had wiry hair and sandals. He was just different. He taught us, 'Form follows function. Before you worry about how it looks, it's gotta work.' He taught us to use our senses. In his Industrial Design class, we carved something that was graded based on how it felt to his sense of touch.

"We designed our own mini space capsule that had to endure simulated reentry into the earth. We had to hold it under a blowtorch for 30 seconds and this little space capsule had to survive the heat.

"He taught us to think about things in a different way. Don't just accept things for what they are."

Mind you, this student is now in his 70's, and if only you could have heard his enthusiasm for Ed, his college professor —fifty years after graduation.

But Ed didn't tell me about his teachings or classes. He spent much of our conversation talking about a new friend, an 11-year-old autistic girl who swims with her father at their local YMCA.

"Her father said that nobody plays with her. But I was committed to making her smile and laugh. I spent twenty minutes playing with her. Nobody else does. They avoid her. I get a kick out of playing with her. I'm an adult. I look different to her. Nobody plays with her but her father. The father works his ass off, carries her around. I don't do that. I just play with her."

"It's like these kids in the gym who are five or six, and when I see them, I'll stop and give them a high five and they all have their hands out. Everyone wants a high five. It takes me fifteen minutes to get through high fiving them all."

"I asked the kids' supervisor, 'How many of these kids have parents?'"

"The supervisor said, 'Not many. They don't have much experience of reacting with adults.'"

Ed continued, "I could hear one kid running after me. He said, 'Mister, are you gonna be back tomorrow?' It broke my heart."

Recently Ed was diagnosed with cancer. He refuses any radiology or chemo.

I asked how much longer he'd like to live.

"I thought I had until the end of the year but I saw the doctor yesterday and he said my numbers are down. I want to make it to my next birthday and then I'll think about it."

He has a lot to live for. He has been married for more than forty years to his second wife who is twenty years younger. She previously had four children and he had three.

After meeting Ed, I felt exhausted because he literally did not stop talking for almost an hour and a half. My questions to him were interruptions. In the moment, I felt impolite to interject. But afterward, I felt uplifted by a man who is here to enjoy the journey.

Just for today, can you, can I, be that person who gives our objectives a break? Instead of "just get me there," can we take a page from Ed's book and focus on making someone smile and laugh? If that was your primary objective each day, to make someone smile and laugh, how might that change things?

It certainly changed that Southwest Airlines flight, which was rough and unpleasant. The wings jerked up and down until just before the wheels touched the runway. My wife and

I breathed a sigh of relief. I wasn't sure if I should ask the person in front of us if they'd like their hair clip and clump of hair that my daughter took from their head.

But then that hilarious Southwest flight attendant chimed in, "Did we land or were we shot down?"

Everyone laughed and we forget about all that turbulence and discomfort. Of the thousands of flights, I remember that one. Of all the teachers in life, Ed is the one remembered by his student.

Maya Angelou said, "Try to be the rainbow in someone else's cloud."

It may sound like the most trivial intention. But it may just be the one that lasts forever.

"I was lucky to have my Grandma Pearl in my life for more than forty years. She lived two weeks shy of her 90th birthday and always inspired me to appreciate the 'finer things' in life. But to her these were everyday things we often tend to overlook— things like the sound of the birds chirping, the color and smell of the lilacs that grew wild in her back yard, the sweet smell of the air just after a summer rain, the feel of the grass between my toes. She was there after my parents' divorce when I was a young eight-year-old. My mother raised me as a working mom in the big city, and it was all she could do just to keep the plates spinning. It was in those young, impressionable years when I spent weekends on Long Island, New York, with Grandma Pearl that my eyes opened to the beauty that was always around us if we take the time to see it. When I take a moment and connect with those things today, I instantly think of Gram and know that she is with me always. Now, being a grandmother myself, I try to instill the same appreciation for those finer things in my grandchildren . . . I want to make sure that in this hurried, over-scheduled, technologically driven, often upside down, crazy world we live in, that they never miss the beauty that surrounds them, and I hope they will always remember me the same way that I remember Grandma Pearl."

—Holly, Los Angeles, California

20

THE HEALING POWER OF
A GREAT STORY

In the Great Stories you know who lives, who dies, who finds love, who doesn't. And yet you want to know again.
That is their mystery and their magic.
—Arundhati Roy, Man Booker Prize winning author

My mom took me to lunch at Eataly in Los Angeles for my 45th birthday. I ordered pizza. She ordered salad. I had a glass of Montepulciano. We talked about my children, her grandchildren. But I couldn't relax. My mom had just gone to the doctor to get a CAT scan for her cough that lingered for many months. The doctor promised to call that same day to share the results of the test. A cloud hung over the lunch. Every time her phone buzzed, we thought it was the doctor. Was she okay?

The older I get, the more my parents, relatives, and friends have these health scares and issues. With aging comes vulnerability. Eventually, death catches up to everyone.

The rest of my birthday, I waited and waited and finally, later in the afternoon, my mom texted to say everything was fine. But the worrying totally consumed my entire birthday. I want my parents to stay young forever. I remember my own grandparents and their process of getting old. Now I see my own parents beginning that process. And hey, at forty-five, I'm no spring chicken. I'm grateful to have had forty-five years with my parents.

And yet, while my parents are 75 and 71, a part of me still feels like a 23-year-old, figuring it all out.

When I ask elders how old they feel on the inside, the response is 10, 11 years old, maybe 35 or 40, but rarely does an elder say they feel their age.

Singer and minister Cora Armstrong said it so perfectly: "Inside every older person is a younger person wondering what the hell happened."

Why does one part of us feel young, while our body decays, and our mind declines? Is there a way to keep it all together, to stay whole?

The most influential elder in my life is Dr. Carl Hammer-schlag, 79. I call him "Dr. H."

I've known him for twenty years. He has been my psychiatrist, my guru. He was the master of ceremonies at my wedding. I was his yoga teacher. We share a passion for the Grateful Dead.

In the 1960s, Dr. Hammerschlag had the typical revolutionary pedigree as a social activist. He was a family doctor who studied at Yale. Instead of going to Vietnam, in 1965, he committed to the Indian Health Service in New Mexico and began work as a family physician with Native Americans.

What he thought would be a few years working with the Native population turned into twenty years.

Dr. H recalls, "Most of what I learned about health and healing came as a result of that exposure. Health was never defined in medical school. In medical school we were experts not in health but in disease. If you weren't sick you were healthy. In Indian country I learned what it meant to be healthy."

In Dr. H's book, *The Dancing Healers*, he describes meeting a man named Santiago who had been admitted to Santa Fe Indian Hospital with congestive heart failure. Santiago was a Pueblo priest and clan chief.

Dr. H walked in the room and saw "an old man in his seventies lying in a hospital bed with oxygen tubes in his nostrils."

Santiago had a beautiful smile and said to Dr. H, "Where did you learn to heal?"

Dr. H rattled off his medical education, internship, certification.

With this beatific smile, Santiago asked, "Do you know how to dance?"

Dr. H said that he liked to dance. He shuffled a bit by his bedside. Santiago chuckled, got out of bed, and short of breath, began to show his dance. He said, "You must be able to dance if you are to heal people."

Dr. H asked, "Will you teach me your steps?"

Santiago said, "Yes, I can teach you my steps, but you will have to hear your own music."

Hear your own music.

Over the twenty years I have known Dr. H, he has taught me, more than anyone, how to hear my own music. It's all about creating sacred space where you can actually listen.

When I went to Dr. H for psychiatry sessions, he would light the sage and say a blessing. As the smoke rose, it created a sense of separation from the rest of the day. We shared a sacred space, ripe for transformation and growth.

On a few occasions, I attended a sweat lodge led by Dr. H for friends and family. A sweat lodge is a Native American purification ceremony. As he describes, "It creates a time and space where you get out of your head. And that's the task in our culture. You've got to find some way to get out of your head. One has to somehow take your head off your shoulders and allow your spirit to breathe, your heart to imagine. Rituals and ceremonies often provide this structure."

I remember the darkness and the heat of the sweat lodge. The conditions force you to face yourself, your issues, your blockages. I didn't handle it so well.

Dr. H said to me, "You've been in a sweat lodge a couple times and you couldn't wait to get out. I remember you crawling under the structure just to escape."

Truth!

"You sit there in the darkness with people you may or may not know and prepare yourself for a cleansing ritual ceremony. To get rid of that cosmic dust that clings to you and keeps you from moving away from the ordinary, the everyday way of seeing . . . and to look at your landscape from a different perspective, from this place of soul and spirit.

"In our culture we don't have a lot of ceremonies anymore that bring people together to share the heart and soul of who they are."

I didn't last for long in the sacred space that is a sweat lodge, but it was long enough to listen and connect with myself. And that is what Dr. H shares about health. It's "being in balance and harmony. What you know in your head and what you say and do by your actions and what you feel in your heart are all telling the same story. Then you're healthy, in balance. The Navajo word for health is 'Hozho,' also the word for 'The Great Spirit,' also the word for truth, beauty, balance, harmony.

"Now there's a concept that's easy to get behind. You can be healthy if what you say is what you mean and what you mean is what you say and what you do is what you say."

That sense of wholeness is Dr. H's superpower. His 6'6" presence, booming voice, powerful intellect, and glowing spirit command my attention. He speaks to every part of my being. He makes me feel whole, at one, reconnected.

And yet, as we get older, there is that sense of fragmentation. A part of you feels forever young and rages against your tiring body and aging mind.

How do we find that wholeness?

Dr. H said, "See yourself as part of bigger picture. The important things are what you leave behind, the stories you tell, your ethical morality and guidelines about how you live on the earth. Our survival as a species is not dependent on transmission of DNA but through transmission of our stories. We need to be telling better stories. We want to listen to the old people because they have stories about how to live that have been recorded for thousands of years, stories that explain the existential questions."

In Indian country, they say if you can tell your story for seven generations, your tribe will survive.

Dr. H shared a story about God going to all the tribes on the earth and asking, "How are you going to guard my Torah? How will you keep it safe?"

The tribes around the planet said, "We will defend it with armies," or "We will put it under the sea," or "We will bury it in vaults."

One tribe says, "Our guardians are our children."

And the Great Spirit says, "Those are good guardians."

But in order for the children to guard the stories, we first must ensure the stories enter into the minds and hearts of the children.

Dr. H continued, "We don't take anything with us. What's really important are the things we leave behind. It's in our stories that we survive."

He suggests a very simple time and place to feel whole and pass along these stories: the dinner table.

"If we restore the dinner meal to a family ritual, we would reduce attention deficit by 90%. Put the phone away and let's sit here at dinner for an hour and talk to each other. Set the stage around the dinner table ritual as a ceremony. This is where we separate ourselves from the day, we talk to each other about what's important, we share our values."

In my household, we "try" to establish dinner as a family ritual. My kids are still young. During dinner, we sit at the table until my three-year-old is climbing under the table and my one-year-old is heaving her plate across the room. There are so many distractions, so many moods to negotiate between my wife and children. Will it get harder or easier as they get older? Only time will tell.

Dr. H shared a great life lesson he learned from Herbert Talahaftewa, a Hopi medicine man. Dr. H was introduced to him as psychiatrist, "a doctor who specialized in the mind."

Herbert turned to Dr. H and said, "What do you know about the mind?"

Dr. H wanted to give him a short, cogent answer but he couldn't figure out how to summarize it. So he said, "What I know about the mind, I can't tell you in a short time."

Herbert responded, "If you can't tell me in a short time, then you don't know it."

At first, Dr. H wanted to be mad. This Herbert reduced his thirty years of education to inconsequence.

Dr. H asked him, "What do you know about the mind?"

Herbert said, "What I know about the mind I can tell you in one word—mysterious."

Dr. H said, "That answer helped me give up the idea that I had to know everything and be able to explain it. We only see parts of the mind. The mind is a multifaceted jewel. As long as you shine a light on it, it reveals different facets. But you have to keep shining the light to illumine those things you have not seen before."

It is the stories we bring to the dinner table, to our family members, to our friends and clients . . . that shine this light. It the stories that will build the bridge between the old and the young.

That being said, I'm sure those of you with older rebellious teenagers are thinking, "Good luck getting your kids to sit and listen to your stories."

But as Dr. H stated, "We need to be telling better stories." So, I will try.

And one more thing from Dr. H that will make a *huge* difference in the stories we tell—don't be so scared of death and dying.

In my life leading up to writing this book, I spent fifteen years teaching yoga, in which Dr. H often was my student. The part of every yoga class that everyone loves is the end, Savasana, which literally means corpse pose. What is yoga without Savasana? It's the most wonderful moment to work toward, when you can lie flat, let go, surrender. It teaches us how to relax into the ending.

And yet, in popular society, we tell a scary story around death, a dangerous story, a story of horror and loss and grief. And of course, death can be all those things.

But as Dr. H said of his very close relationship with his children, "The greatest advantage of having a multi-generational family is that your grandkids see you live—and die—in a way that allows it to be discussed. In our culture anything that has to do with death and dying is anathema. Our family talks about everything. We laugh. It's good!"

My family doesn't talk enough about death. When I sat with my mom at my birthday lunch, I kept thinking to myself, "What if the doctor has a scary report for her? What if she dies?"

And I made myself a nervous wreck worrying about death, to such an extent that it took away the very occasion we were there to celebrate—a new year of *life*!

It happens way too often. We tell a certain story about aging and death that is not the story we want to be telling or living. It's a story we assume old people will share, and it may be a reason some of us avoid talking to our elders in the first place.

I hope the stories in this book will remind you that when people are approaching death, it is actually a really beautiful part of life, filled with wisdom and history and insight, and best of all, a sense of mystery about what's yet to come.

Philosopher Søren Kierkegaard said, "Life can only be understood backward. But it must be lived forward."

As we continue with our hustle, our focus, our grind . . .

May we make time for the stories from our elders.

May we make time to ask.

May we make time to listen.

May we make time to share these stories with our children.

EPILOGUE

In almost every elder, I have seen and heard something ageless. It's the part of you which always and forever loves mocha almond fudge ice cream, and the sound of Chopin (or Jerry Garcia), and being outside on a warm summer night.

Florence, 96, told me how she recently completed a road trip with her boyfriend (who is eight years younger). They drove from California to Minneapolis, stopping along the way to check out the Tetons and Mt. Rushmore. Once arriving in Minneapolis, they flew to Nova Scotia for a visit. They listened to a tape of country music with "Kenny something" as their soundtrack. Rock on, Florence!

Sydelle, 86, says every day to her Amazon Echo, "Alexa, play Chopin" and it brings her back to the time when she was a little girl. Her father would come home from his job at the factory, turn on the old radio, and they would listen together to classical music. Now she is losing her eyesight and feeling her age, except when she hears the music.

Helen, 101, says, "I don't think about how old I am. The first thing I do is get up and do my exercises, sit ups, and touch my toes."

Margaret is working on becoming a comedienne and screenwriter, at 88 years young!

Ann, 76, retired and moved to Alaska to volunteer for the National Park System. She said, "Don't retire from something. Retire to something."

Let there be no doubt, these elders are feeling their age. They are mourning a recently deceased spouse, or struggling with the pain of bad knees, or the confusion of a fading memory, or all of the above. And yet, the ageless part of them rages "against the dying of the light." They have so much to live for!

Take a moment to imagine yourself at 94-years-old. Just pretend . . .

You still have the same passion for the music you love, the comfort food you crave, the friends who put your mind at ease. At 94, your ageless self is alive and well.

But at 94, you don't hear as well. Your eyes are not so great. You had a knee and hip replaced. Your spouse died recently and your heart is heavy. You love your grandchildren but they don't come to see you as much as you would like. So you're lonely.

And yet, that ageless part of you won't quit. Not only that, the ageless part of you continues to dream. That is something I learned toward the end of writing this book: You never stop dreaming.

Irmgard, 91, never had children and lives alone at a retirement home in Salt Lake City. She dreams that someone will take her to the opera before she dies.

Eily, 85, dreams that the younger generations will be nicer to each other than their parents have been to their fellow human beings (note to self).

Atha, 99, dreams of getting her writing published or at least reading her writing in front of an audience.

Think again about the 94-year-old version of you. You are holding something in your heart, a dream that never saw the light of day. You want so badly to release it, to set it free.

At 94, you might not have the energy or the resources to fulfill your dream. You're just hoping to have enough to take a walk outside, let alone embark on an adventure. But if the dream starts to sink instead of rise, it can drag you down with it.

Actor John Barrymore said, "You don't age until your regrets outnumber your dreams."

So let's focus on the dreams. Now, tomorrow, and especially when you get older.

There are two questions I did not ask when interviewing people for this book.

"Do you have a dream you wish to fulfill before you die?" And "Can I help you fulfill that dream?"

These are two questions I will ask forevermore.

Of all the life lessons I have learned from the elders, this is my favorite:

Stop asking people about their age and start asking about their dreams.

YOUR STORY

If you have a story from your 80, 90, or 100 years of history, or if you know an elder whose story you'd like to share, go to www.davidromanelli.com/elders. You will find a place to post a story and photo, and I will do my best to help get your message and story out there. Let's continue to ensure that the older and younger generations are growing closer.

This is an ongoing discovery and you can find more life lessons from the oldest and wisest at the following:

Instagram: @WiseElders
Facebook: @WiseElders
Web: www.DavidRomanelli.com/elders

ACKNOWLEDGMENTS

I would like to thank the Search and Care organization which was the spark that ignited my passion in this area. You introduced me to so many beautiful individuals who are part of this book. Brian Kravitz, Robin Strashun, Leland Pitts, Herbert Duran, Dana Pirulli, Laurie Ballentine Ferris . . . I have the greatest admiration for the hard work you do to ensure that our older neighbors age with dignity and love.

To my wife. I feel so lucky to share this journey with you. You teach me the most important life lessons about loyalty, patience, respect, and love. I am so excited to watch Remo and Cooper grow, to solve challenges, to create a beautiful life, their life, and to savor it all together. When I take my final breath, may we be holding hands, surrounded by our children, grandchildren, and great-grandchildren—watching the Dodgers win the World Series! I love you so much.

To Leah Zarra, for the long process of bringing this book to life. You have answered 10,008 questions and just hung in there with me. Thank you.

To Tony Lyons, for catching my Hail Mary in 2013.

To my parents, for being the most awesome, loving parents who keep showing up for me and my children and my wife through every stage of life. I love you so much.

To my sister-in-law, Candice, and brother, Darren, and my nieces, Auggie and PhePhe, may we all grow old together and celebrate health and happiness every single year in an exotic, amazing place. Everyone gets to create the soundtrack . . . Guns & Roses AND Phish!

To my stepparents, Luana and Dave, both mentioned in this book, who opened completely different dimensions of what it means to have a healthy, loving, nurturing relationship. I am so grateful to you and for you.

To Kate, Kirk, and Kiel, I enjoy every moment we spend together—in Hawaii, the Grand Canyon, hiking Camelback, and putting up with me as a houseguest. Your grandchildren will be so lucky to inherit even a fraction of your values and attitude and work ethic.

To Carrie and Mark, Amy and Barry, Ethan, Micah, Sam, Eliana, Andrew, may we see each other more and more as we get older. That's on me! You continue to show me the true meaning and power of "family."

To the most impactful elder I ever met, Katherine, the 111-year-old in NYC who inspired my last book, whose story I have told countless times, and whose resilience, humor, and *joie de vivre*, together, are my favorite formula for happiness.